Indian Knowledge System in Higher Education Context

(ISBN: 978-93-7421-694-1)

Authors

Dr. Priya Rao
Dr. Nitin M Rane
Dr. VedVyas Jayaprakashnarayan Dwivedi
Ms. Kamakshi Vedvyas Dwivedi

SAI INFO SOLUTION

"Press & Publication"

Title: Indian Knowledge System in Higher Education Context

ISBN: 978-93-7421-694-1

Authors: Dr. Priya Rao, Dr. Nitin M Rane, Dr. VedVyas Jayaprakashnarayan Dwivedi, Ms. Kamakshi Vedvyas Dwivedi

Address: Office No 708 & 709 , 7th floor, Bhasker Adroit, Pandit colony, Sharanpur Road, Nashik, Maharashtra, India 422002

Branches : Pune | Noida | Hyderabad | Bangalore | Goa | Chennai

Call : 090968 13348

Email: sai.info2009@gmail.com

Website: https://saiinfosolution.co.in

Contents

Chapter 1 - Introduction to Indigenous Knowledge and Education Reform

The integration of Indigenous Knowledge Systems (IKS) into contemporary higher education is at once a paradigmatic shift and a reassertion of epistemic agency. As education systems worldwide recognize the necessity of decolonizing knowledge paradigms and celebrating intellectual pluralism, India's civilizational heritage, based in multilingual traditions, holistic philosophies, and experiential modes of knowing, uniquely places it to spearhead such a shift.

Indian indigenous knowledge is not primitive or marginal; it is an in-depth, contextual, sophisticated, and ethically sound epistemology that covers metaphysics, logic, medicine, politics, arts, and ecological ethics. These are traditions fostered over centuries in varied linguistic, regional, and oral forms that provide integrative schemes rather than reductionist ones, and value-founded logic rather than merely mechanistic thought. That holistic quality makes IKS a system that combines intellectual rigor with cultural and ethical context.

But the colonial intellectual heritage systematically excluded these knowledge systems from participation in the new intellectual order, deeming them as unscientific or antiquated. By favoring Eurocentric knowledge systems, the heritage brought about a deep disconnection between schooled pedagogy and indigenous people lived experiences. Such estrangement has not merely dissolved cultural identity but also dismantled indigenous intellectual capital, leaving generations to inherit a disconnected sense of their epistemic inheritance.

Today's educational reforms hold the promise of mending this gap. The National Education Policy (NEP) 2020 has officially acknowledged the importance of indigenous epistemologies and has invited their systematic incorporation into curricula, pedagogy, and research culture. This vision promises more than tokenism. It demands situating IKS in a manner that enhances cultural identity, encourages sustainable thought, and advances comprehensive learner development. By linking educational objectives with the overall goal of inclusive and contextually sensitive knowledge construction, these reforms open the doors to an authentically pluralist academic space.

IKS is a broad array of fields, all interconnected by a philosophy of knowledge as lived, shared, and ever-changing. These fields synthesize India's oral, experiential, and scholarly traditions in an integrated vision for education.

Figure 1 below is a representation of the layered evolution from Indigenous Pedagogies to Holistic IKS Pedagogy, exemplifying the interconnected flow of adaptation, integration, and immersion:

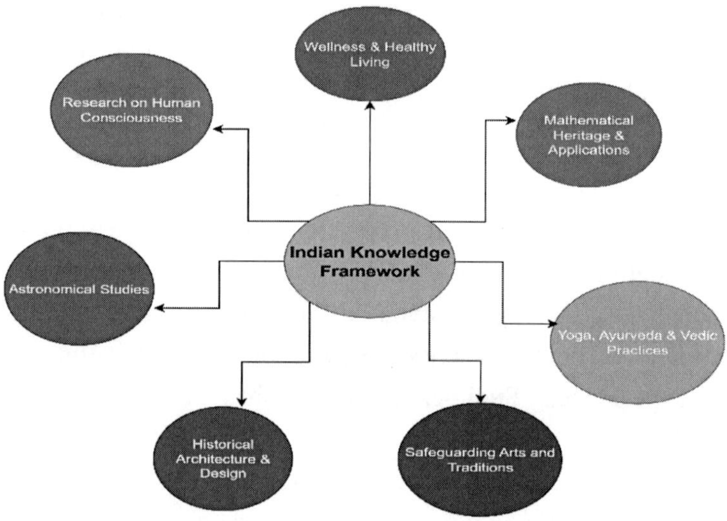

Figure 1. Core Domains of the Indian Knowledge Framework

The Indian Knowledge Framework (IKF) represents an integrated synthesis of ancient wisdom, scientific investigation, and cultural heritage. As the figure shows, the framework covers a wide but linked field of knowledge, representing the multidisciplinary character of India's intellectual heritage. Wellness & Healthy Living focuses on holistic health practices based on indigenous nutrition, lifestyle, and preventive medicine.

Mathematical Heritage & Applications recognizes India's historical contributions to mathematics and contemporary applications. Yoga, Ayurveda & Vedic Practices promote tried and tested modes of health, philosophy, and spiritual growth. Conservation of Arts and Traditions preserves and rejuvenates performing arts, crafts, and oral traditions. Historical Architecture & Design depicts architectural wonders and design concepts consistent with ecological well-being. Astronomical Studies identifies India's ancient astronomical achievements and their impact on international science. Research on Human Consciousness discusses the philosophical and subjective investigations of the mind, perception, and being.

- **The Rationale for IKS Integration**

The incorporation of Indigenous Knowledge Systems (IKS) into formal schooling is more than a superficial cosmetic exercise in curriculum change; it is a deep civilizational necessity to restore harmony to the global knowledge order. This transformation is rooted in an awareness that there are various, equally relevant systems of knowledge—ones that are situated in particular localities, informed by environmental realities, shaped by historical pathways, and fostered by cultural traditions. Such systems of knowledge are not merely "alternative" in a marginal way; they are on a par epistemologically with hegemonic, frequently homogenized, Western systems and ought to have an institutional voice alongside them.

IKS are intergenerational, relational, and experiential. They arise from long-term human interaction with natural and social worlds over centuries to answer the needs, aspirations, and moral systems of given societies. The diversity of IKS is striking, embracing subjects ranging from astronomy to agriculture, architecture, philosophy, medicine, and linguistics. Historically, they have done more than just guarantee the survival of communities; they have positively influenced adaptive resilience, allowing societies to respond to changes in the environment, social change, and cultural disruptions with creativity and unity.

The rationale for incorporating IKS into formal education can be explained by four interrelated and synergistically reinforcing pillars: epistemic justice, cultural continuity, pedagogical diversity, and sustainability.

1. **Epistemic justice:** is based on the intellectual and moral obligation to reclaim, authenticate, and legitimize forms of knowledge that have been marginalized. Such a process actively confronts epistemic hegemony built through colonial and post-colonial institutions, which for centuries have undervalued or silenced indigenous voices.

2. **Cultural continuity:** emphasizes the imperative to safeguard and pass on identity-defining practices, languages, and worldviews. It ensures that education acts as a vehicle of cultural affirmation instead of being a force for alienation or assimilation, thus allowing future generations to inherit a consistent sense of self and heritage.

3. **Pedagogical diversity:** acknowledges that the learning processes are not uniform. Indigenous pedagogies, which have their origins in oral histories, apprenticeship paradigms, observation, and learning through

participation in rituals, are holistic, context-based, and embodied forms of education that can enhance and even revolutionize mainstream teaching methods.

4. **Sustainability**: both environmental and social, requires contextual know-how. Most of the know-how lies in indigenous ecological values, local community land stewardship, and governance arrangements that have supported ecosystems and societies for millennia.

As Bharucha (2023) rightly asserts, the revival and reintegration of IKS in curricula is no scholarly fancy. It is a deliberate act of resistance to the structural and cultural loss caused by homogenizing epistemologies. It is a summons to re-ground education in lived experiences, nurturing resilience, diversity, and relevance in the context of global crises.

- **Displacement of Indigenous Epistemologies in Colonial Education**

The colonial era in India was a deliberate and systematic displacement of Indigenous Knowledge Systems (IKS). It was not just material domination, but a deliberate discrediting of the native epistemologies, an intellectual subjugation that found deep penetration into language, pedagogy, cosmology, and cultural self-awareness. It was not merely a byproduct of modernization; instead, it was inherent in the very structure of colonial rule, which aimed to determine what was "rational," "scientific," and "modern" and to exclude and marginalize the colonized's knowledge forms.

Nineteenth-century education reforms institutionalized an Anglocentric curriculum centered on utilitarian and bureaucratic education, perfectly in line with the administrative requirements of the colonial state. This curriculum negated the significance of holistic, pluralistic, and spiritually integrated systems of knowledge that were at the core of Indian intellectual traditions. The Gurukula model derived from the guru–shishya parampara was a highly personalized and intensive form of learning. It synthesized ethical development, environmental literacy, philosophy, literature, sciences, and arts into a unified whole. Under the colonial regime, this system was systematically eliminated, pushed into oblivion, or transformed into a symbolic relic instead of a living pedagogical practice.

This change was not just a curricular reform but a re-ordering of epistemological hierarchies. Oral traditions, indigenous languages, medical systems like Ayurveda, Siddha, and Unani, and advanced philosophical systems like Nyāya and Advaita were disallowed. They were substituted with an exam-based pedagogy with emphasis on rote memorization, fractured disciplines, and the acquisition of utilitarian knowledge aimed at creating clerks and administrators instead of independent thinkers or integrated scholars.

The outcome was an epistemological break of immense depth—a break with the civilizational continuity of knowledge. Generations of students became disengaged from their intellectual inheritance, inheriting in their place a system which devalued their ancestors' wisdom. The break went beyond the destruction of information; it encouraged a cultural alienation of greater depth since the colonized started internalizing hierarchies of value forced upon them, and often viewed their traditions with inferiority-tainted eyes nurtured by colonial schooling.

This displacement had long-lasting effects that were extended into the postcolonial period. Long after political independence, knowledge transmission frameworks retained much of their colonial features, and there were continuing problems in recovering and renewing Indigenous epistemologies as living, dynamic systems relating to modern society.

▪ The Role of NEP 2020 and Emerging Educational Policies

The National Education Policy (NEP) 2020 represents a paradigmatic shift in the trajectory of education in India. For the first time in post-independent policy, it formally recognizes the worth of India's rich intellectual traditions and the need to incorporate Indigenous Knowledge into the curriculum. NEP 2020 demands a "reinvigoration of the Indian education system with its roots in Indian ethos." NEP 2020 suggests the integration of Sanskrit, regional knowledge traditions, Vedic mathematics, Ayurveda, and Indian logic systems as major curricular elements across school and higher education.

Furthermore, it fosters multidisciplinary, mother-tongue teaching and total learning paradigms that are in tandem with the pluralistic character of IKS. The policy invites universities to partner with grassroots holders of traditional knowledge, e.g., artisans, tribal chiefs, and village elders, thereby institutionalizing avenues for grassroots epistemologies to gain entry into the mainstream.

New educational policies that come after NEP 2020 also place a premium on experiential learning, environmental literacy, and social-emotional learning, all of which strongly align with the Indigenous worldview, which understands knowledge as an embodied, ethical, and relational process. This provides new horizons for envisioning pedagogy not just as the delivery of content but as epistemic engagement.

To delineate the extent of this transformation, the following table contrasts the colonial educational legacy with the IKS-aligned policy directions articulated in NEP 2020:

Table I. Colonial vs. NEP 2020 IKS Educational Dimensions

Dimension	Colonial Legacy	NEP 2020 & IKS Direction
Language of Instruction	English-dominant, Sanskrit erasure	Multilingualism, Sanskrit revitalization
Curriculum	Eurocentric, fragmented	Holistic, Indian-centric
Knowledge Sources	Western canon, exclusion of oral traditions	Textual + oral + experiential knowledge
Pedagogy	Rote learning, teacher-centered	Experiential, learner-centered
Epistemology	Rationalist/empiricist only	Integrative, pluralistic

- **Reclaiming India's Epistemic Legacy in Higher Education**

Reclaiming India's epistemic heritage in higher education is both a symbolic and structural imperative. Symbolically, it returns dignity to epistemologies that have been devalued or wiped out. Structurally, it mandates curricular decolonization, faculty development, resource creation, and institutional collaboration with traditional knowledge holders. Universities need to transform themselves from knowledge-consumption to knowledge-generation centers, particularly in the area of indigenous sciences, technologies, and philosophies.

Reform of higher education has to go beyond tokenism to working frameworks with the creation of research institutes, digital archives, inter-university schools on IKS, and multilingual production of knowledge. Indian aesthetics, classical logic, ancient jurisprudence, traditional ecology, and spirituality courses have to be academically equivalent to Western-origin courses.

In addition, reclaiming epistemic heritage also entails epistemological humility recognizing that there are many legitimate world views and that knowledge is improved through dialogue between traditions, rather than the hegemony of one. The knowledge economy in the 21st century, if based on India's civilizational systems of knowledge, can be both innovative as well as inclusive.

***

Chapter 2 - Philosophical Foundations of Indian Knowledge Systems

The intellectual origins of Indian Knowledge Systems (IKS) draw upon one of the world's most ancient and richest intellectual traditions in which knowledge is not just seen as information but as a metaphysically powerful force that informs the formation of individual consciousness as well as collective concord. Learning in IKS goes way beyond the mere acquisition of facts; it is a profoundly integrative process that fosters moral character, intellectual distinction, spiritual sense, and experiential wisdom. Rooted in the Indic worldview, this tradition values the unity of existence, the interdependence of all life forms, and the quest for truth (satya) as the ultimate human aspiration.

The center of this intellectual inheritance is the Darshanas, the six ancient schools of Indian philosophy, that is, Nyaya, Vaisheshika, Samkhya, Yoga, Purva Mimamsa, and Vedanta. Although each expresses a distinct vision of reality, human destiny, and the path to liberation (moksha), they are also highly interrelated, presenting complementary views of the nature of existence. These streams of philosophy together constitute an elaborate fabric of metaphysics, epistemology, and ethics, offering a unified basis for comprehending the self, society, and the universe.

Also fundamental is the Pramana doctrine, the theory of legitimate means of knowledge, which outlines how one determines truth. Valid pramanas are considered to be direct perception (pratyaksha), logical inference (anumana), authoritative testimony (shabda), comparison (upamana), postulation (arthapatti), and non-perception (anupalabdhi). This epistemological scheme ensures that investigation is stringent, systematic, and rooted in rationality as well as experience.

Shastraic schools like Nyaya and Mimamsa further reinforce this intellectual framework by honing instruments of logical inquiry, dialectics, and systematic text interpretation. With their careful approach, these schools preserve the rigor and discipline of inquiry so that philosophical discourse is not vacuous speculation but a methodical pursuit of openness and reality.

In the academic world, these philosophical foundations inform curriculum and pedagogy. They prompt students to question, reason ethically, and reflect, developing higher-order thinking along with creativity and context-dependent problem-solving capabilities. This orientation equips students to deal with contemporary complexities while being anchored in eternal wisdom.

Finally, the philosophical underpinnings of IKS express a vision of schooling as a holistic and redemptive process, one that reconciles intellectual excellence with ethical orientation, cultivates inner development as well as outward success, and connects personal transformation with the larger welfare of society and nature.

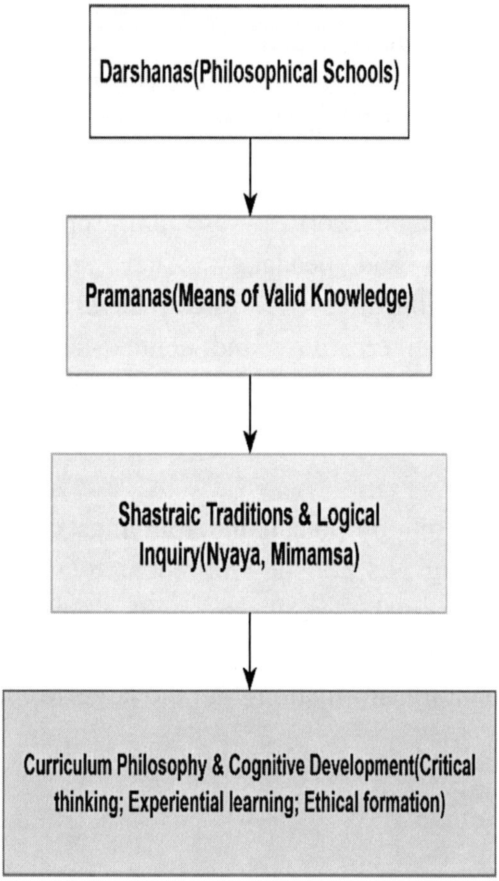

Figure 2. Interrelation of Darshanas, Pramanas, and Curriculum Outcomes

- **Darshanas and Indic Epistemology**

The Darshanas are the philosophical foundations of the Indian Knowledge Systems (IKS), being organized forms of "seeing" or "experience" of reality. Darshana means literally "vision" or "point of view," and this indicates that Indian philosophy is not purely speculative but is an experiential science of direct realization of truth. Six orthodox (āstika) schools, Nyāya, Vaiśeṣika, Sāṃkhya, Yoga, Pūrva Mīmāṃsā, and Vedānta, are the foundation of classical Indian philosophy. Each offers a unique metaphysical schema, epistemological process, and spiritual goal, but all seek ultimately the aim of satya (truth), tattva (reality), and mokṣa (liberation).

None of these schools is a complete system; they frequently overlap in concepts, methodology, and goals. Nyāya places great reliance on logical analysis and systematic thought as the means of distinguishing truth from falsehood. Vaiśeṣika is concerned with classifying the material and non-material factors of reality. Sāṃkhya offers a dualistic metaphysics of Puruṣa (undiluted consciousness) and Prakṛti (material nature), whereas Yoga develops on the basis of Sāṃkhya to provide an applied science of self-control, intellectual concentration, and religious knowledge. Pūrva Mīmāṃsā offers advanced methods of textual analysis to establish dharma, while Vedānta, particularly Advaita, delves into the non-dual nature of the self (Ātman) and the absolute reality (Brahman).

The epistemology of India, born out of these Darshanas, believes that true knowledge (pramā) not only has to be true but also dispel ignorance (avidyā) and promote human flourishing. Knowledge is incomplete if it is unaccompanied by ethical living and spiritual development. The recognized pramāṇas (means of knowledge) are perception (pratyakṣa), inference (anumāna), and authoritative testimony (śabda), with others including comparison (upamāna), postulation (arthāpatti), and non-cognition (anupalabdhi). This broad scope sets Indic thought apart from much Western epistemology, where ethical or religious ends tend to be divorced from evaluation of knowledge.

Educationally, the Darshanas stimulate a curriculum that prioritizes questioning intelligence, dialogic interaction, and integration of intellectual understanding with moral and experiential wisdom. This integrated vision educates learners who are not merely knowledgeable but also self-aware, ethically sound, and socially responsible. By interlacing metaphysical investigation, logical severity, and experiential practice, the Darshanas provide a timeless model for cultivating well-rounded individuals who can balance personal growth with collective good.

- **Pramanas: Means of Valid Knowledge**

In the Indian Knowledge Systems, Pramāṇa, which is based on the Sanskrit root pramā (true knowledge) and the suffix ṇa (instrument), refers to the instrument by which knowledge is acquired in a trustworthy manner. The analysis of pramāṇas serves as the basis for Indic epistemology since it identifies not just what may be known, but how it may be known to be certain. In contrast to purely abstract categorizations, the pramāṇa system synthesizes logical acuteness, experiential confirmation, and moral direction so that knowledge gain remains meaningful, reliable, and transformative.

Classical Indian philosophy identifies a differing number of pramāṇas among the various Darshanas. The Nyāya tradition speaks of four perceptions (pratyakṣa), inference (anumāna), comparison (upamāna), and verbal testimony (śabda). The Mīmāṃsā school adds two more to make six, postulation (arthāpatti) and non-cognition (anupalabdhi). Buddhist epistemologists tend to insist on only perception and inference, whereas other traditions follow more selective approaches in consonance with their ontological assumptions.

1. **Perception (Pratyakṣa)**: is regarded as the most immediate form of knowledge, resulting from the collision between sense organs and external objects without any conceptual distortion. It is also divided into ordinary perception (laukika) and extraordinary perception

(alaukika), with the latter comprising yogic or intuitive insight.

2. **Inference (Anumāna):** Develops on perception to create knowledge of the unseen by reasoning. It works on the premise of a universal relation (vyāpti) between observed signs and concluded implications, such as in concluding fire from smoke.
3. **Comparison (Upamāna):** Knowledge acquired by analogy or similarity, and it performs an important role within linguistic understanding and classification.
4. **Verbal Testimony (Śabda):** Recognizes the validity of trusted sources, like the Vedas or the words of reputed persons, emphasizing the function of tradition and linguistic conveyance in maintaining cultural knowledge.
5. **Postulation (Arthāpatti):** Resolves seeming contradictions by taking an explanatory hypothesis, like assuming unseen actions to explain seen outcomes.
6. **Non-cognition (Anupalabdhi):** Affirms the absence as a valid object of cognition, enabling identification of what is not present.

What characterizes the Indic method of pramāṇas is its refusal of a rigid hierarchy between sensory and non-sensory knowledge. Rather, it encourages a context-specific choice of means befitting the field of inquiry, empirical, metaphysical, or ethical. This approach shields both against blind faith and untrammelled skepticism by maintaining balance between verification and receptiveness to transcendental realities.

In pedagogy, the theory of pramāṇa influences teaching by provoking students to think through various ways of knowing: observation, critical thinking, textual hermeneutics, and contemplative cultivation. In such integrative processes, cognitive flexibility is promoted, so that learning becomes more than simply the transmission of information but the development of discernment (viveka) and the capacity for applying what is known to benefit individuals and society.

- **Shastraic Traditions and Logical Inquiry (Nyaya, Mimamsa)**

The śāstraic tradition of India includes the codified knowledge systems that inform intellectual, ethical, and spiritual investigation. These śāstras, philosophical texts, linguistic texts, ritual texts, law texts, and art texts, are far from dogmatic doctrines; instead, they are dynamic systems of knowledge maintained by intense debate and commentary. The Nyāya and Mīmāṃsā schools are especially noteworthy in developing the logical and hermeneutic foundations of Indian knowledge systems.

Nyāya, sometimes referred to as the "science of reasoning," is committed to the investigation of logic, epistemology, and the method of debate. It describes knowledge as the perception of an object as it is and formulates rigorous rules for correct reasoning. Nyāya logic embraces syllogistic patterns, analyses of fallacies, and methods of analysis to settle controversies. Nyāya's merit consists in codifying reasoning as a systematized art so that philosophical investigation will be well-ordered and fact-based.

Mīmāṃsā, focused mostly on Vedic interpretation, evolves a complex theory of language, meaning, and authority. It insists that the Vedas are eternal and authorless and hence an infallible source of dharma-knowledge. By elaborating hermeneutics, Mīmāṃsā scholars established guidelines for the interpretation of subtle and sometimes contradictory scriptural statements. Methodological exactness from this tradition impacted religious discourse as well as legal and ethical reasoning in the Indian tradition.

Together, Nyāya and Mīmāṃsā represent complementary methodologies of investigation Nyāya on reason, from experience and evidence, and Mīmāṃsā on textual exegesis and interpretive coherence. Both emphasize reasoned argumentation, intellectual integrity, and the judicious elimination of fallacy.

In the academic arena, combining Nyāya and Mīmāṃsā principles with academic studies will enable students to become sharper in reasoning, better interpreters, and more capable of engaging in civil yet critical discussion. These enhance both analytical acuity and cultural competence, linking medieval logic to modern problem-solving capability.

- **Implications for Curriculum Philosophy and Cognitive Development**

The epistemological and philosophical foundations of the Indian Knowledge Systems have deeper implications for curriculum development and mental growth. Fundamentally, these systems look at education as a process of transformation, not merely for the acquisition of information but for the development of wisdom, moral intuition, and self-knowledge. In contrast with strictly utilitarian conceptions of education, the Indic tradition focuses on the balanced development of intellect (buddhi), feeling (manas), and moral will (dharma).

The pramāṇa and darshanas system promotes a multi-dimensional pedagogy. For example, combining perception (pratyakṣa) and inference (anumāna) in the teaching of science leads to empirical robustness, and with the inclusion of śabda as authoritative testimony, cultural and historical grasp is strengthened. Logical argumentation from Nyāya can be used in mathematics, debates, and critical thinking practice, while interpretative approaches from Mīmāṃsā can be used in the study of language, literature, and law. Such cross-disciplinary flexibility means that the students are provided with both analytical and interpretative skills.

From a cognitive standpoint, such a curriculum promotes metacognition, thinking about thinking. Training in the pramāṇa system habituates students to critically assess sources, probe arguments, and detect biases. Study of the śāstraic tradition breeds patience, depth of thought, and respect for orderly dialogue. Notably, the incorporation of ethical inquiry as a part of epistemology develops moral reasoning in tandem with intellectual prowess.

In the contemporary situation, where education tends to favor the swift processing of information, the Indic model reminds us that teachers need to reconcile speed with depth, and utility with sense. An Indic-based curriculum would result in graduates who are not only informed but discriminating, compassionate, and able to synthesize a variety of viewpoints. This comprehensive growth conforms to current aspirations of education for global citizenship, where flexibility, critical thinking, and moral accountability are essential.

***

Chapter 3 - Curriculum Innovation and Transdisciplinary Design

The changing needs of higher education in the twenty-first century call for a departure from discipline-based learning to integrative, transdisciplinary models that promote holistic awareness, problem-solving ability, and cultural competence. In this context, the inclusion of Indian Knowledge Systems (IKS) in mainstream academic curricula presents itself as both an intellectual necessity and a strategic initiative. By systematically integrating the philosophical, scientific, and practical aspects of IKS across various disciplines, ranging from the sciences, technology, engineering, mathematics, humanities, and social sciences, curriculum development can move beyond traditional silos and develop a more integrated knowledge ecosystem.

Innovation of the curriculum in this field is more than the addition of content, but it calls for structural thinking about course structure, credit systems, and pedagogical approaches. It asks that classic epistemologies be reconciled with modern academic organization, with the result that native frameworks are contextualized for current issues but without compromising their conceptual integrity. This enhances cognitive diversity, enhances cultural grounding, and makes it possible for learners to navigate world knowledge systems without sacrificing local intellectual tradition depth.

Transdisciplinary design is the working framework for this convergence, stimulating interactivity between domains to develop new applications and approaches. It leverages cross-field synergies from disciplines like Ayurveda and biomedical sciences, Vastu Shastra and green architecture, Jyotisha and astronomical calculation, Ganita and data analysis, and Arthashastra and contemporary economics. The aim is not only to safeguard heritage knowledge but to positively reimagine its contribution to the solution of today's societal and technological challenges. Through the integration of IKS into transdisciplinary curricular models, higher education institutions can produce graduates who are not just specialists, but adaptive thinkers capable of responding to complex, interrelated global issues.

- **Mapping IKS onto Modern Academic Disciplines**

The systematic linking of Indian Knowledge Systems (IKS) to present-day academic fields is an important step towards the integration of indigenous epistemologies into present-day schooling. IKS is a vast body of philosophical, scientific, aesthetic, and practical knowledge developed over millennia, including areas such as Ayurveda, Vastu Shastra, Jyotisha, Ganita, Arthashastra, ancient linguistics, musicology, and ecological conservation. Mapping these systems requires situating conceptual equivalences, methodological intersections, and thematic resonances between IKS and dominant disciplinary frameworks in STEM, social sciences, and the humanities. For example, Ayurveda can be mapped against biomedical sciences, pharmacology, and wellness studies, and Jyotisha provides intersections with astronomy, mathematics, and cultural history.

Both epistemological sensitivity and methodological rigor must be employed to do so. In contrast to simple translation of ideas, mapping requires one to respect the ontological paradigms underpinning IKS, e.g., cyclical time, relational ecology, and integrative wellness, that sometimes contrast with prevailing Western paradigms. Cross-referencing allows for the identification of parallel innovations, distinct problem-solving strategies, and different understandings of knowledge production. For instance, the spatial concepts of Vastu Shastra can be translated into architectural design and environmental psychology, and Ganita's algorithmic techniques have homologies with computational mathematics and data sciences.

The intellectual benefit of such mapping is in facilitating curricular inclusivity, intellectual pluralism, and research collaborations in multiple disciplines. By integrating IKS into conventional academic taxonomies, universities can design hybrid spaces of knowledge that facilitate critical discourse rather than cultural tokenism. In addition, this integrated process can spur innovative pedagogy in which students interact with both the historical richness and the present-day relevance of IKS. Finally, mapping is the pioneering act in transdisciplinary curriculum construction, making sure that ancient knowledge is not relegated to heritage preservation but feeds into global knowledge systems.

- **Designing Credit-Linked IKS Courses Across STEM and Humanities**

The incorporation of Indigenous Knowledge Systems (IKS) within higher education curricula needs to have a well-planned design that not only crosses disciplinary boundaries but also operates within the credit-based framework of newer academic courses. A well-established design needs to be able to both sustain the epistemic integrity of IKS as well as connect it meaningfully with contemporary disciplinary frameworks. This entails mapping points of intersection between IKS fields and recognized fields of study, capturing learning outcomes that are both responsive to indigenous epistemologies and universally recognized scholarly standards, and taking on pedagogies that facilitate critical and reflective work with alternate knowledge traditions.

Credit-linked IKS courses must be modular so that they can be easily integrated within undergraduate and postgraduate courses without causing disruptions in prevalent curricular formations. Modularization also facilitates the provision of flexibility in terms of duration, intensity, and thematic orientation, so that courses from basic surveys to specialized advanced levels exist. Every module must bear a fixed credit point, corresponding to contact hours, assessment strategies, and practical activities like field immersion, ethnographic research, or project-based implementation.

A successful implementation plan would include interdisciplinary teaching teams with a mix of IKS practitioners and subject-matter specialists from STEM and Humanities fields. This team model guarantees that classic knowledge is framed with the latest research, promoting intellectual cross-pollination and methodological plurality. The evaluation framework should strike a balance between theoretical understanding and experience-based learning, so that students not only acquire conceptual frameworks but also build applied skills for their respective fields.

By integrating IKS courses into formal credit systems, institutions are able to turn indigenous knowledge into a pillar of formal learning from a supplementary or elective module. This integration allows for a dialogic interaction between tradition and modernity, enhancing the educational experience with views that are locally based but internationally relevant.

- **Integrating Ayurveda, Vastu, Jyotisha, Ganita, and Arthashastra**

Incorporating Ayurveda, Vastu, Jyotisha, Ganita, and Arthashastra into the school curriculum offers a multi-disciplinary framework for integrating Indian Knowledge Systems (IKS) into modern education. Each of these areas represents centuries of empirical experience, codified theory, and practical applications that can be mapped against contemporary academic disciplines. For example, Ayurveda's focus on preventive health and harmonious living finds echoes in biomedical sciences, public health, and environmental sustainability. Vastu Shastra provides architectural concepts grounded in space harmony and energy maximization, applicable to civil engineering, urban planning, and design courses.

Jyotisha, which includes astronomy and astrology, offers a double opportunity for learning, combining observational science with cultural heritage. Ganita, ancient Indian mathematics, includes algebra, geometry, combinatorics, and trigonometry, which are both pure and applied science requirements. Arthashastra, an ancient book on economics, politics, and statecraft, has political science, economics, and management education connections.

By methodically correlating these systems of knowledge to contemporary disciplines, institutions can craft interdisciplinary courses that are compliant with academic credit structures and cultivate cultural literacy. This also keeps IKS content from being delivered as singular heritage information but as a living, dynamic knowledge base. The table below highlights the academic intersections:

Table II. Core Domains of Indian Knowledge Systems (IKS) and Their Modern Academic Integration

IKS Domain	Core Focus	Modern Academic Integration
Ayurveda	Preventive healthcare, lifestyle sciences	Biomedical sciences, public health, nutrition
Vastu Shastra	Spatial harmony, energy flow in design	Architecture, civil engineering, urban planning
Jyotisha	Astronomy, cultural astronomy, astrology	Physics, astronomy, cultural studies
Ganita	Algebra, geometry, combinatorics	Mathematics, computer science, data analytics
Arthashastra	Governance, economics, strategic planning	Political science, economics, business administration

Embedding these domains into the curriculum not only strengthens interdisciplinary learning but also bridges cultural heritage with cutting-edge research, enabling a holistic and globally relevant education model.

- **Models for Transdisciplinary Knowledge Fusion**

Transdisciplinary knowledge integration is the systematic integration of concepts, methods, and frameworks across several disciplines to work through problems on a comprehensive level. Transdisciplinary models do not simply move between or among subjects, which are often retained in multidisciplinary or interdisciplinary efforts; rather, they break out of these and establish new frameworks of inquiry. This method is especially well adapted to the integration of Indian Knowledge Systems (IKS) into modern-day STEM and humanities education because it makes possible the co-evolution of ancient wisdom and contemporary scientific logic.

The following models can be utilized for successful transdisciplinary integration:

1. **Thematic Integration Model**

   This model is built around a unifying theme that serves as an intellectual anchor for course planning. The theme, e.g., Sustainable Living, Wellness and Society, or Technologies of the Future, is the center around which various subjects are integrated. For instance, a Sustainable Living course could just as well combine Ayurveda's holistic principles of health, environmental science's evidence-based ecological analysis, sociology's community-based development schemes, and public policy's institutional frameworks. This thematic intersection enables students to realize a concept not by itself, but as an interdependent system, wherein cultural heritage and contemporary innovations call upon and support one another.

2. Problem-Centric Model

Here, the point of departure is a real-world problem specific, frequently intricate, like climate change adaptation, food security, or urban resilience. In tackling climate change, for example, the curriculum could incorporate Vastu Shastra's orientation and spatial organization principles to minimize heat load within buildings as well as existing energy-efficient building technologies. The process of learning is problem-solving and hands-on, challenging students to find ways that ancient wisdom can augment or support engineering, economic, and environmental solutions. This is a highly useful model for applied disciplines, as it develops concrete problem-solving capability while being sensitive to cultural heritage.

3. Co-creation Model

This framework stresses co-creation of knowledge among various stakeholders, traditional knowledge specialists (e.g., Ayurveda vaidyas, Vastu professionals), academic researchers, and practitioners from industry. Within this integrated setting, traditional methods are tested, reformed, and sometimes even reinterpretated based on current needs. For instance, the creation of a public health policy may consist of incorporating Ayurvedic health indicators in combination with biomedical data analytics to provide both cultural salience and scientific validity. Co-creation closes epistemological divides, thus providing the outcome frameworks with greater inclusivity, local relevance, and usability.

Within IKS, such models promote students and researchers to combine native methodologies with evidence-based contemporary methods. For instance, Ganita's algorithmic solution methods can be combined with computer science for constructing effective computational models, and Arthashastra's principles of governance can be integrated into current policy analysis models.

The transdisciplinary paradigm also fosters methodological pluralism through the encouragement of both qualitative and quantitative approaches. This guarantees that ancient philosophical models are experimented with, adjusted, and implemented in contemporary settings. Eventually, such models not only add to academic scholarship but also equip students to function effectively in multicultural and fast-paced global settings.

Through the incorporation of transdisciplinary fusion into curricula, schools can build innovation, critical thinking, and cultural adaptability, such that ancient wisdom and contemporary science are co-creating future knowledge systems.

Businesses now have an alternative to implementing ERP thanks to cloud computing. Businesses save a great deal of money with it. Data security is one of the main barriers to the adoption of cloud ERP. This worry has been heightened by reports of credit card and personal customer data security breaches at major online retailers. The good news is that, as of right now, they are not aware of any particular instance in which a cloud ERP provider's sensitive data was compromised. Nonetheless, businesses have expressed concern that storing operational and financial data in the cloud raises the risk of disclosing private information to other parties and hackers.

***

Chapter 4 - Pedagogical Transformation and Teaching Models

The integration of Indigenous Knowledge Systems (IKS) with contemporary higher education requires a shift in pedagogical thinking—one from mere tokenism to a fundamental rethink of pedagogical and learning systems. Ancient Indian education systems, as represented by the Gurukula model and the Shravanam–Mananam–Nididhyasanam (listening, reflection, and meditation) triadic process of learning, hold deep, tried-and-tested insights for integral education. These systems place greater value on individualized mentorship, moral and ethical development, practical integration of theory, and self-knowledge alongside academic learning. Informed by particular cultural and philosophical backgrounds, these pedagogies support relational learning, character education, and value inculcation, enriching technical expertise with moral acumen.

But the modern systems of higher education are working under strains of scalability, standardization, accrediting needs, and technology infusion. Here, strongly individualized, context-dependent pedagogies risk being sidelined or reduced. The core challenge lies in upholding the epistemic and ethical density of IKS without making it conform to credit-based modularization and globally applicable curricula. Careful pedagogic innovation is needed where oral cultures, experiential learning, and dialogic methods are articulated into modern academic frameworks.

For example, Ayurvedic field immersion, Vastu Shastra architectural observation, or ethnobotanical research can be reconceptualized in multidisciplinary research paradigms, combining empirical verification with conventional epistemologies.

These models may yield double value: preserving the integrity of indigenous traditions while guaranteeing their academic legitimacy in global paradigms.

Technology is capable of being a bridge between old traditions and new demands. Cyber museums, interactive simulations, and multimedia repositories are able to conserve threatened oral histories, recreate cultural ceremonies, and disseminate indigenous learning worldwide across geographical boundaries, as well as institutional ones. Hybrid models of learning—mixing face-to-face mentorship with cyber platforms—can be both scalable and authentic.

Language is fundamental to protecting the philosophical richness of IKS. Sanskrit, Pali, and Prakrit are not just linguistic instruments but conduits for entire worldviews, taxonomies, and ontologies of knowledge. Their judicious incorporation into higher learning, reinforced by accurate translation, annotation, and contextual explication, protects the conceptual integrity of IKS from being diminished by modernization.

This chapter surveys a variety of pedagogical models that blend the philosophical depth of indigenous knowledge with the reach and adaptability of modern education. By combining traditional wisdom with innovation, it offers an implementable model for the incorporation of IKS in global academia—upholding cultural fidelity, scholarly rigor, and global relevance.

- **Indigenous Pedagogies: Gurukula, Shravanam-Mananam-Nididhyasanam**

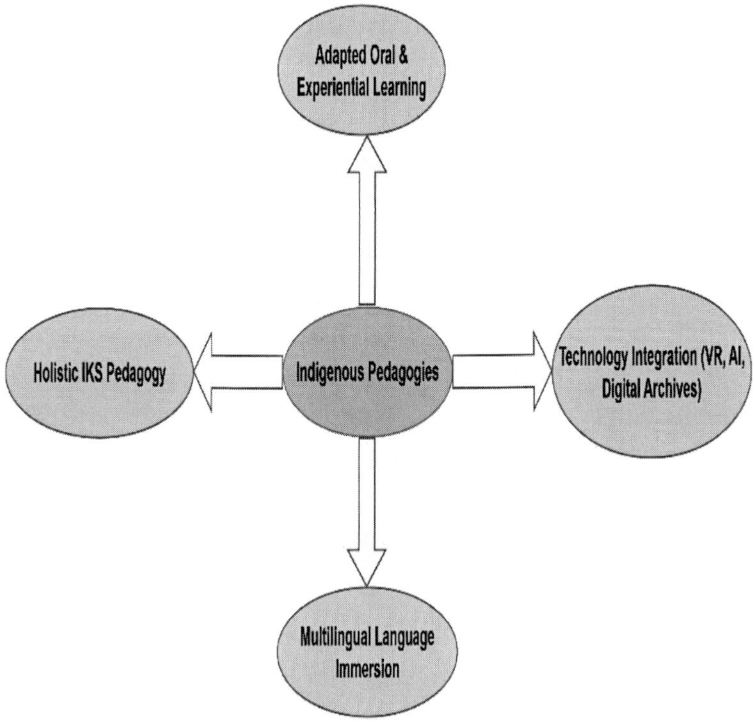

Figure 3. Integration Model of Indigenous Pedagogies in Contemporary Education

The Gurukula system was not simply a system of instruction; it was a saturating cultural institution in which the learning, living, and formation of character were all interwoven. Under this system, pupils—shishyas—lived with their teacher, the guru, frequently for long periods. This residential model established a consistent and close environment for learning in which education spilled outside the confines of lessons in the classroom and into the arenas of everyday life, spiritual practice, and moral behavior. The guru-shishya relationship rested on trust, respect, and responsibility, representing the best kind of mentorship. Such an intimate connection enabled the instructor to adjust teaching to the learner's intellectual development, moral orientation, and life goals, thus ensuring not only academic competence but also life readiness in general.

Central to this tradition of teaching was the Shravanam–Mananam–Nididhyasanam paradigm, a three-step procedure that cultivated learning as a dynamic, tiered process. Shravanam was intense, focused listening to teaching, whether oral recitation, scriptural explanation, or narrative. Mananam involved thoughtful reflection, in which students examined critically, questioned, and assimilated the knowledge, checking it against their own rationality and experience. Nididhyasanam symbolized the meditative absorption of wisdom, with the intellectual understanding becoming embodied. This cyclical method discarded mechanical memorization in favor of knowledge transubstantiation, where learning was a fundamental aspect of one's worldview and behavior.

The Gurukula paradigm was highly oral and conversational. Instead of passive reception, students participated actively in questioning, debates, and reinterpretation of teachings. Instruction went beyond textual reading to encompass ritual practices, engagement with nature, and practical skills to ensure learning was experiential and values-based. Ethical formation (sadācāra) here was not an independent moral subject but organically integrated into all learning processes—content and character were fused from the very beginning (Sen et al., 2025)

For institutions today, this legacy has deep lessons. Modifying the Gurukula and Shravanam–Mananam–Nididhyasanam model for use today demands education reform centered once more on contemplative practice, ethical foundations, and mentorship—values most attenuated in mass-delivery, standardized systems. With technology integrated, mentorship can be carried out across spatial distance through computer platforms, video conversations, and online mentorship rooms. Curricula might be organized into recursive cycles: didactic listening (lectures, readings, or multimedia lessons), reflective engagement (peer discussions, journals, or group analyses), and experiential internalization (hands-on projects, field immersion, or contemplative exercises).

Such a model is not only consistent with the agendas of 21st-century holistic education but also recovers the humanistic richness of indigenous pedagogy. By situating ethics, empathy, and mindfulness at the center, it makes sure that students are not only provided with technical proficiency but are also informed by wisdom derived from lived experience.

- **Contemporary Adaptation of Oral, Experiential, and Dialogic Learning**

Historical Indian pedagogies gave centrality to oral transmission, experiential learning, and dialogical discussion as root learning processes. Oral pedagogy acknowledged the living nature of knowledge: narratives, metaphors, and parables imparted sense beyond literal words. Experiential pedagogy welcomed embodied learning, students learned through active participation in rituals, observation of practice, and apprenticeship under master teachers. Dialogic pedagogy, exemplified by Shastrartha (philosophical discussion), formed thinking, listening, and argumentation faculties through structured dialogue.

Modern education can innovate these ways to deepen engagement. Oral learning can be retained through storytelling, case-based learning, and live demonstrations, even if mediated through digital platforms. For instance, a live cooking demonstration of a traditional Ayurvedic dish can display holistic health principles in a sensory, memorable manner. Experiential learning can occupy field work, community immersion, maker labs, and studio practices, allowing students to relate theory to everyday contexts. Dialogic learning can flourish with the help of seminar discussions, peer panels, mock debates, and online forums, instructing students to express, criticize, and polish ideas in groups.

These adaptations will have to be scaffolded within contemporary curriculum frameworks. Teachers will have to construct learning cycles: initially expose learners to demonstration or narrative, subsequently provide scaffolded practice and reflective debriefing. They can be helped in retention and insight by digital tools such as video portfolios, reflective journals, and peer feedback applications. Tests will have to change as well: no more solely written tests, but oral presentations, embodied demonstration, and reflective essays.

This integration rekindles learning as active and relational, not passive. It reiterates meaning-making, fosters ownership, and develops critical thinking through lived experience. By incorporating oral, experiential, and dialogic traditions into contemporary classrooms, even in digital form, they instill depth, relevance, and inquiry into learning.

- **Blending Technology with Traditional Pedagogies**

The insertion of technology into established pedagogical models provides a compelling means of developing systems of education that are at once culturally embedded and future-oriented. Traditional models like the Gurukula system place a high value on mentorship, moral formation, and hands-on education, while contemporary technology makes available tools for broadening access, enriching experience, and diversifying the pathways through which knowledge is accessed. The task and the challenge are to synthesize these models without sacrificing the integrity of either.

Technology emerges as an enabler in a hybrid model, not a substitute. For instance, oral, conversational interactions typical of classic learning can be complemented by digital conferencing facilities that link learners and guides across distances, without sacrificing the one-to-one or small-group closeness. Digital interactive repositories can hold oral traditions, ritual customs, and cultural lore, allowing students to return to them time and again, an extension of Shravanam today. Virtual and augmented reality can re-create classical learning spaces, from ashram areas to natural habitats, so that learners can immerse themselves in environments that can no longer be physically accessed.

The individualization inherent in classical pedagogy also resonates with adaptive learning platforms. These can gauge a student's readiness and adjust resources to match, imitating the guru's function of adapting instruction to the learner's speed. Exercise in reflection, previously guided face-to-face, may be done via online journaling programs, threaded discussion forums, or template self-assessment software. In this manner, Mananam reflection still maintains profundity but enjoys the accessibility of asynchronous participation.

Most importantly, combining technology with tradition is not simply a question of digitizing information but of safeguarding the human relationships, ethical basis, and integrated development that characterize traditional systems.

For Nididhyasanam, internalization of knowledge technology can facilitate contemplative practice in the form of guided meditation apps, AI feedback on skill performance, or even biometric instruments that assist learners in tracking attention and well-being. But these should be so used as to enhance, not hamper, the learner's inner journey.

Effective integration hinges on careful design. Educational systems must integrate cultural stories, values, and rituals into their interfaces and sequence of learning. Measures must assess not just cognitive performance but also ethics, empathy, and resilience. In this synthesis, technology enhances tradition, and tradition ensures that technology benefits human and cultural flourishing. The outcome is an educational model that respects the knowledge of the past but prepares learners for the challenges and opportunities of the future.

- **Role of Language (Sanskrit, Pali, Prakrit) in Teaching IKS**

Language constitutes the heart of passing and conserving Indian Knowledge Systems (IKS), not as a means of communication alone but as a keeper of cultural memory, philosophical richness, and conceptual accuracy. Three ancient languages of the Indian subcontinent, Sanskrit, Pali, and Prakrit, are essential to comprehend the epistemological and methodological context of IKS. Every one of them comes with different intellectual traditions, textual bodies, and semantic structures that are essential for understanding the true meaning of concepts, practices, and values rooted in India's civilizational tradition.

Sanskrit, popularly referred to as the "language of the gods" (devavani), has been the major vehicle for encoding Vedic, Upanishadic, and an immensely diversified range of scientific, literary, and philosophical works. Its precision in grammar, rooted in Panini's Ashtadhyayi, allows for nuanced expression and logical clarity, enabling the formulation of abstract principles with minimal ambiguity. For teaching IKS, Sanskrit serves not only as a linguistic channel but also as an intellectual discipline that trains the mind in structured thinking. Exposure to original Sanskrit texts helps learners engage directly with foundational sources, avoiding distortions that may arise in translation.

Pali, the Tipitaka language of Theravāda Buddhism, is instrumental in conveying Buddhist philosophy, ethics, and monastic norms. The Pali Canon (Tipitaka) is a treasure trove of insights into epistemology, meditative psychology, and moral philosophy. Learning IKS through Pali scriptures promotes learning about ethical systems, mindfulness-based pedagogies, and humanistic modes of learning. Further, the less complex grammatical structure of Pali, as opposed to Sanskrit, makes it accessible and yet maintains the philosophical depth.

Prakrit languages, consisting of a set of vernaculars spoken in ancient and medieval India, played a significant role in democratizing knowledge. Several Jain scriptures, folk tales, and local knowledge traditions are etched in many Prakrit dialects. Prakrit acted as the link between scholarly elite discourse and common usage, rendering philosophical and moral teachings available to broader sections of the public. Its presence in IKS pedagogy emphasizes the merit of inclusiveness and cultural diversity in education.

In IKS pedagogy, combining these languages extends beyond linguistic skill; it builds sensitivity to the cultural and historical situation in which knowledge arose. Learners acquire the capacity to read into concepts their original semantic field, promoting richer understanding and critical thinking. In addition, the multilingual strategy mirrors the pluralistic ethos of Indian civilization, inviting respect for diversity and situating learners in common intellectual traditions. By integrating Sanskrit, Pali, and Prakrit into IKS pedagogy, education continues to be authentic, intellectually challenging, and culturally continuous, and the traditional wisdom continues to be pertinent and vibrant for generations to come.

***

Chapter 5 - Research Methodologies Rooted in IKS

Indian Knowledge Systems (IKS) have a long tradition of systematic inquiry. These traditions blend observation, experience, and philosophical thought. IKS research is not merely about knowledge construction. It is also concerned with cultural wisdom preservation. It balances empirical data with ethical responsibility. Current research tends to follow Western paradigms. These are epistemology-specific. They hold objectivity, quantification, and replicability in high esteem. IKS research, however, holds both concrete and abstract aspects in high regard. Knowledge is tried in life, in communities, and over generations.

Decolonizing research involves shedding narrow academic silos. It involves letting indigenous epistemologies lead the way. It ensures research questions derive from the community. It also ensures results are pertinent to the people researched. Ethics are not an add-on. They are integral to the method. Observation in IKS is holistic. The healer can observe not just the symptoms of the patient but also the environment, diet, and emotional state. The astronomer can observe the stars as well as the cycles of seasons and cultural rituals. These are then related to codified Shastric (text-based) principles.

Field narratives are unique. They keep track of oral tradition, local legend, and lived experience. Action research enables people to co-produce knowledge. It builds confidence and helps the findings to be followed up. Combining Anubhavic (practical) and Shastric (scriptural or theoretical) research creates equilibrium. Practice provides practical wisdom. Shastra guarantees relevance to tried-and-true wisdom. Together, they yield research that is innovative and rooted.

The New Education Policy 2020 (NEP 2020) promotes the inclusion of IKS in academia. This chapter investigates how researchers can implement IKS principles in contemporary projects. Emphasis is given to four areas. First, a decolonizing approach and taking up ethical, community-driven practices. Second, Indian ways of using evidence, observation, and inference. Third, action research and field stories as instruments of co-creation. Fourth, experiential and Shastric knowledge integration in research design.

IKS approaches are not a matter of substituting Western science. They are a matter of broadening the research landscape. They permit a variety of ways of knowing. They promote respect for contextual considerations. They produce research that is more inclusive, relevant, and enduring. In the pages that follow, each of these themes is fleshed out in detail. The aim is to lead scholars and practitioners to apply IKS not as a topic of research, but as a living, dynamic methodology.

- **Decolonizing Research Methods: Ethics and Epistemology**

Decolonizing knowledge starts with reframing the question of who determines knowledge. Research in colonial frameworks tended to be for outside agendas. It took information without yield for the community. In IKS, knowledge generation is mutual. The researcher benefits from the community, and the community benefits from the results.

Ethics within IKS are based on dharma. This is not just a matter of moral codes. It is a responsibility to maintain balance, truth, and respect. Each step in research, from question development to publication, must be in concordance with this responsibility. Consent is more than a formal agreement. It is a reciprocal relationship of trust.

Epistemology in IKS holds multiple forms of knowing in high esteem. Knowledge is textual, oral, visual, or experiential. Each has an equal claim to validity. It stands in opposition to Eurocentric paradigms that tend to favor written records. Oral histories are saved not merely as narratives but coded caches of scientific, historical, and ecological knowledge. Decolonization is also a matter of changing the research agenda. Subjects are not imposed externally. They arise from within the society. The research seeks to answer actual needs, not theoretical lacunae. This makes the findings relevant and actionable.

In practice, this translates to participatory planning. Local leaders, elders, and practitioners are involved from the beginning. Their insights inform the design. Their input refines the process. This avoids misinterpretation and minimizes cultural bias. Language is also essential. Community language is employed in IKS research. Ideas are articulated in terms that are meaningful to the culture. This prevents distortion that can occur in translation. It also ensures the retention of indigenous words, which have embedded meanings that are lost in other languages.

Methodologically, decolonizing research is flexible. Instruments may be interviews, rituals, observation, and textual analysis. Each instrument is tailored to the context. For instance, a study of a medicinal plant could involve both botanical identification and traditional medicine practices. The product is rigorous and culturally valid research. It resists the hegemony of one world and worldview over others. It produces a common space where academic and indigenous approaches complement each other.

Finally, decolonizing research is not a single event. It's an ongoing process. It needs humility, respect, and being open to learning. It transforms the way knowledge is acquired, understood, and utilized. It makes certain that IKS is a living system, not merely a textbook subject.

▪ Indian Approaches to Evidence, Observation, and Inference

Evidence in IKS is not limited to quantitative information. It encompasses what may be observed, heard, felt, and sensed within context. Observation is multilayered, consisting of sensory awareness blended with cultural interpretation. An Ayurvedic physician, for instance, does not merely record symptoms; he or she notices body language, emotional tone, seasonal context, and the environment of the patient's life. This extensive, integrative observation facilitates holistic comprehension. In traditional Indian philosophy, evidence (pramāṇa) is divided into direct perception (pratyakṣa), inference (anumāna), verbal testimony (śabda), comparison (upamāna), presumption (arthāpatti), and non-cognition (anupalabdhi). They are all valid means of reaching truth, and they are all used as and when the situation demands.

Direct perception is seeing and hearing with disciplined attention. It is not effortless observation but trained perception. Farmers interpret cloud formations, soil texture, and bird flight to forecast rain. Metalworkers assess the quality of metal based on tone and color when heated. These are not arbitrary techniques; they are developed through experience and apprenticeship. Inference is an extension of perception. A doctor may infer internal imbalance from slight outer signs. A naturalist can forecast animal migration based on observed plant flowering cycles. This is empirical and experiential reasoning.

Verbal report is similarly appreciated, especially when it is from credible, capable agents like elders, teachers, or ancient texts. These agents are not followed blindly; they are honored for gathered wisdom and experimented with lived life. Comparison and analogy are learning and explanatory tools. A teacher may describe a complicated celestial phenomenon by comparing it to a common seasonal phenomenon. Presumption bridges gaps where direct evidence is missing, enabling warranted conclusions to be tested subsequently. Non-cognition acknowledges the fact that lack of evidence can itself be evidence, like the silence of birds preceding a storm.

IKS combines these approaches in a context-sensitive, adaptable way. A single inquiry could use direct perception, inference, and testimony together. This multi-layered reasoning yields solid conclusions that are still contextual. In contrast to most contemporary approaches, which disconnect qualitative and quantitative data, IKS keeps them together. Numbers, stories, and natural signs are all part of the body of evidence. The result is a research process that is dynamic, comprehensive, and responsive to complexity. This process guarantees that knowledge is not abstracted from reality but rooted in lived, unbroken experience.

- **Action Research, Field Narratives, and Community Co-creation**

Action research within the IKS approach is neither an external initiative set upon a people nor a population. It arises from the community's continuous practice and requirements. The researcher is not a detached person who "researches" others but becomes a participant who helps in achieving the aims of the community. It is a cyclical process with action, observation, reflection, and re-action, each stage guided by both indigenous and modern knowledge systems. Practical problem-solving is the goal, with immediate applicability, rather than a theoretical product.

Field stories are a key part of this process. They are not anecdotal narratives. They are formal accounts of process, events, and experience, thick with cultural allusions and practical information. A story about a growing season could involve precipitation patterns, seed choice, pest management techniques, and ritual practices. Any single detail may have embedded ecological and social knowledge. These stories are documented, not only in text, but in sound, image, or symbol, and they capture tone, gesture, and environment.

Community co-creation makes research outputs the property of the people whose knowledge made them possible. The community is engaged right from the start, defining the problem, shaping the method, gathering data, interpreting findings, and determining how to use them. This avoids the extraction of knowledge for no benefit. It also makes sure that findings are used in a manner compatible with local ethics and aspirations. Co-creation redefines research as a partnership rather than a hierarchical exchange.

The techniques employed in this kind of study could involve participatory mapping, shared workshops, collaborative experimentation, and mutual documentation. These processes generate trust, enhance accuracy, and facilitate innovation grounded in local reality. Both-directional knowledge flow occurs. The researcher contributes tools, structures, and possibly technical capabilities. The community provides contextual depth, lived knowledge, and adaptive practice.

The product is durable knowledge production. It not just addresses current concerns but also enhances the community's capacity to deal with future issues. It solidifies cultural pride, maintains oral traditions, and makes indigenous contributions more visible in broader academic and policy arenas. Action research in IKS is thus not merely an approach but also a dedication to justice, equity, and the survival of multiple forms of knowledge.

- **Integrating Anubhavic (Experiential) and Shastric Research**

IKS does not accord experience (anubhava) and scripture or textual tradition (śāstra) equal but rival sources of knowledge. Rather, it synthesizes them in perpetual conversation. Experiential knowledge is formed by lived action in the world, farming, healing, building, teaching, navigating, and legitimized by repeated success. Shastric knowledge is derived from codified texts Vedas, Upanishads, Puranas, and classical scientific treatises, which retain condensed wisdom and theoretical principles. Both are needed. Theory unaided by experience may be narrow in application. Experience unaided by theory may become irrelevant.

Synthesis starts with an awareness of the mutual worth of both sources. A common metallurgist might understand by experience how to mix an alloy. A shastric text might say why, because of certain proportions and heating techniques, it will succeed. When put together, these viewpoints fortify both knowledge and practice. In the same way, a farmer may use observation to adjust seed choice in addition to adhering to lunar planting schedules outlined in agricultural śāstras. This balance of observation and principle forms a flexible, responsive base of knowledge.

The integration process is cyclical. New experiences are compared to known shastric truths. If findings match, the tradition is reaffirmed. If findings diverge, the divergence is analyzed in detail. Occasionally, new experiential discoveries create a reinterpretation of texts. Occasionally, textual understanding leads to novel forms of practice. This lively exchange keeps the knowledge system vibrant and dynamic.

Methodologically, the incorporation of anubhavic and shastric research necessitates instruments capable of processing both empirical and textual evidence. Field experiments, interviews, and participatory observation accompany textual analysis, translation, and commentary. The researcher might record the apparent effects of a medicinal plant, and afterward, contrast them with recipes in Ayurvedic classics. Differences are not rejected but probed to reveal context alterations in the environment, variation in plant species, or variations in human constitution over time.

The outcome is a rich and balanced method of research that respects tradition but accommodates contemporary needs. It escapes the sterility of entirely theoretical learning and the fragmentation of entirely experiential try-and-error. By interlacing the dignity of śāstra and the flexibility of anubhava, IKS retains its ability to produce efficacious, sustainable, and culturally embedded knowledge. This unification guarantees that wisdom is at once timeless and timely, acting as an animating guide for communities in transition.

***

Chapter 6 - Technology-Driven Dissemination and Digital Archiving

The preservation, renewal, and sharing of Indigenous Knowledge Systems (IKS) in the 21st century need a thought-out integration of cultural heritage principles and cutting-edge technological potential. Traditionally, IKS developed through oral histories, community-based apprenticeship systems, and place-based pedagogies situated within local contexts. Although these processes fostered authenticity and intergenerational stability, the intensifying forces of globalization, digital connectivity, and socio-cultural shifts have intervened in and deconstructed many conventional transmission avenues. Issues like loss of indigenous languages, degrading mentor–disciple bonds, and physical degradation of manuscripts, artefacts, and ritual sites call for innovative, scalable, and sustainable methods that guarantee both preservation and renewability in modern settings.

Technology-based interventions hold unprecedented potential to protect and revive IKS. Digital preservation now allows systematic preservation of manuscripts, oral traditions, artifacts, and ritual acts using high-resolution imaging, metadata-dense cataloging, and cloud-based storage. Not only do these archives preserve vulnerable heritage, but they also make it accessible to scholars, practitioners, and communities globally. The combination of Machine Learning (ML) and Artificial Intelligence (AI) takes this process to the next level by allowing semantic mapping, where texts from ancient times are algorithmically matched against contemporary science and culture studies such as ecology, linguistics, governance, and medicine. This revolutionizes archives from being static containers of information into dynamic, interactive knowledge systems that can uncover patterns and meanings lost in isolated records.

Immersive media technologies, Extended Reality (XR), that is, Virtual Reality (VR), Augmented Reality (AR), and Mixed Reality (MR), are transforming the experience of audiences with heritage. VR simulates sacred places, history, and traditional practices in interactive, three-dimensional space, providing an embodied experience of cultural immersion. AR superimposes indigenous stories, symbols, and linguistic notes on physical spaces, enriching both tourism and educational experience. MR environments bring these advantages together, allowing students to learn through authentic practices in simulated but contextually relevant spaces.

In addition, interactive learning environments expand IKS dissemination through gamified pedagogies, adaptive learning patterns, and multimedia-dense narration. These environments maintain the spirit of shastric traditions but transpose them into present-day educational paradigms without compromising cultural continuity or relevance to younger generations. Open-source infrastructures then open up access further, facilitating transnational cooperation where communities, researchers, and custodians of culture enrich the IKS corpus together.

Technologically mediated dissemination and storage, in other words, are not necessarily preservationist acts—although they are preservationist acts, they are acts of cultural revival. By blending old epistemologies and new digital technologies, societies can turn IKS into a dynamic, changing, living resource that connects past knowledge and future innovation and ensures its passage to yet unborn generations.

- **AI/ML Applications in Grantha Digitization and Semantic Linking**

Ancient Indian manuscripts in Grantha, Devanagari, and other scripts are both a technical and a cultural challenge to digitize. High-resolution scanning of manuscripts ensures the physical aspect is captured, but to be converted into a machine-readable, searchable, and semantically enriched form, top-of-the-line artificial intelligence (AI) and machine learning (ML) methods are needed. Conventional Optical Character Recognition (OCR) software tends to struggle with scripts of historical periods because of anomalous glyph shapes, ink deterioration, and contextual orthographic variability. More recent breakthroughs in deep-learning-based OCR systems, particularly convolutional and transformer models, have shown great potential in properly recognizing and reconstructing text in deteriorated or elaborate manuscripts.

After digitization, semantic linking becomes a priority. Artificially intelligent natural language processing (NLP) models, trained on Sanskrit, Prakrit, Tamil, and other ancient corpora, can recognize thematic trends, philosophical classifications, and intertextual allusions between manuscripts. For instance, a semantic engine may automatically link a verse from a Grantha manuscript on Ayurveda to its corresponding commentary in a medieval Tamil palm-leaf manuscript or connect an astronomical calculation to its usage in modern physics pedagogy. Such interlinking not just spans time frames but also allows researchers to move through a multidimensional web of indigenous knowledge.

Machine translation algorithms, especially those that combine neural sequence-to-sequence architectures, provide additional opportunities by translating ancient writings to contemporary Indian languages and English without diluting philosophical subtlety. Combined with entity recognition tools trained to recognize shastric categories like Nyaya logic concepts or Charaka Samhita medical recipes, AI makes it possible to develop semantically labeled, cross-referenced storage.

Aside from scholarly research, AI/ML-based semantic linking can fuel educational software. For example, students learning environmental science may be able to access indigenous ecological principles through AI-compiled cross-references to manuscripts of Vrikshayurveda. This converts static repositories into living resources adaptable to contemporary curricula.

Yet, the ethical aspect is crucial. Algorithmic openness, cultural sensitivity in metadata tagging, and indigenous data sovereignty principles must inform every phase of AI implementation. Systems need to be developed in collaboration with linguistic researchers, indigenous knowledge keepers, and digital archivists to ensure that digitization not only preserves the textual material but also its epistemological and cultural integrity.

In effect, AI and ML are not technical tools in the Grantha digitization process, they are facilitators of an active semantic web that re-links disconnected knowledge traditions, making them searchable, understandable, and meaningful in today's world.

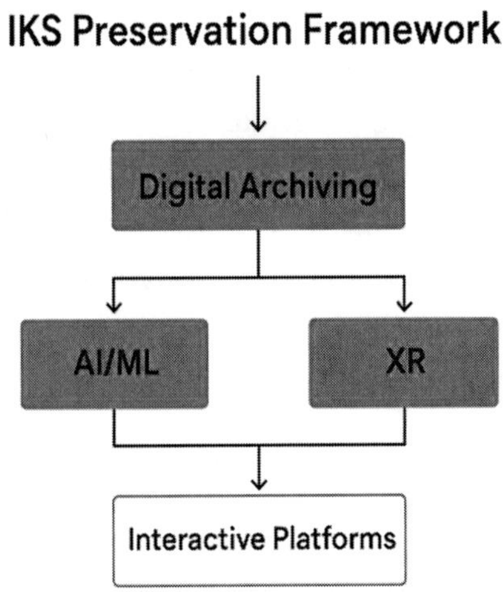

Figure 4. IKS Preservation Framework

- **Virtual Museums, XR Simulations, and Digital Repositories**

Virtual Museums, Extended Reality (XR) simulations, and digital repositories have become revolutionary tools for transforming the sharing and conservation of Indigenous Knowledge Systems (IKS). Beyond static displays or conventional archives, these digital entities provide evolving, interactive, and multisensory experiences that involve viewers in ways that traditional methods cannot. Virtual museums make it possible to have digital exhibitions curated with rare manuscripts, artefacts, and intangible cultural expressions that can be accessed anywhere in the world, dispelling geographical and temporal limitations. Virtual space facilitates layered storytelling, integrating textual accounts, multimedia, and 3D reconstructions, to place artefacts within their historical, social, and philosophical context.

XR technologies such as Virtual Reality (VR), Augmented Reality (AR), and Mixed Reality (MR) expand this ability through fully immersive experiences that enable learners, researchers, and culture lovers to live through heritage on-site. An instance is the use of a VR recreation of an ancient Shastric debate to rebuild the atmosphere of an ancient gurukula with setting details and interactive exchanges, thus enhancing contextual insight and emotional connection. AR, however, has the potential to enhance actual-world heritage sites or manuscripts with overlaid annotations, semantic connections, or reconstructions of missing content, presenting hybrid learning experiences that bridge the physical and virtual worlds.

The coupling of these immersive platforms with sophisticated AI-based annotation and metadata creation further increases the interpretability and accessibility of digital heritage. Clever systems are able to automatically create semantic links between manuscripts, artifacts, and associated cultural histories, allowing users to navigate knowledge streams previously siloed or unavailable. Digital repositories are the foundation of such systems, providing secure storage, indexing, and retrieval functions that maintain long-term preservation and universal accessibility.

Studies highlight the role of XR technologies in cultural heritage, especially in maximizing user experience, retention of learning, and cross-cultural interactions. As Innocente et al. (2023) point out, immersive XR architectures in the context of cultural heritage not only conserve artefacts in a digital form but also reinterpret them in ways meaningful to today's audiences, thus cultivating preservation as well as innovation. Their research offers a systematic framework to include XR tools within heritage workflows to ensure scalability, accessibility, as well as cultural responsiveness.

By integrating IKS into virtual museums, XR simulations, and networked repositories, knowledge custodians can break away from preservation into dynamic revitalization. This process redefines heritage as a fluid, dynamic resource that speaks to digital-native generations while still being rooted in authenticity.

- **Interactive Platforms for Shastric Learning**

Shastric education, based historically in oral transmission, memorization, and dialectical reasoning (samvada), must be adjusted in order to flourish in digitally mediated spaces. Interactive interfaces can potentially maintain the intensity and richness of shastric pedagogy while opening it to a worldwide audience.

Contemporary platforms can mimic the layered nature of shastric learning, wherein basic texts (sutras) are read with authoritative commentaries (bhashyas) and sub-commentaries (tikas). Computer interfaces can enable simultaneous, side-by-side viewing of these layers, hyperlinked terms linking to lexical databases, etymological origins, and connected passages in various shastras. AI-based natural language processing enables real-time breakdown of elaborate Sanskrit compounds, providing grammatical and contextual sense.

Gamification features, be it interactive quizzes over Nyaya logic, simulated Vedic rituals, or argument spaces for Mimamsa interpretations, can keep the learner active without compromising intellectual discipline. Audio-visual records of traditional recitations, virtual whiteboards, and collaborative annotation software can assist in participatory learning where students can engage directly with expert teachers and fellow students worldwide.

In addition, immersive features such as VR-based reconstructions of classrooms can recreate the feel of a classic gurukula, with ambient sound, spatial layout, and sequential flows of learning. Interactive case studies can be presented as well, such as using Ayurvedic diagnostic techniques to hypothetical patient cases or reconstructing astronomical models from texts in Jyotisha.

To provide inclusivity, platforms can offer multilingual assistance, facilitating primary content in Sanskrit or local languages to be accompanied by translations and elucidation in commonly spoken world languages. Adaptive learning algorithms can vary in complexity according to the learner's preexisting knowledge so that beginners and learned scholars equally benefit.

Ethical and cultural concerns need to continue to be at the core of platform design. The depiction of shastric traditions needs to be reviewed by subject matter experts and lineage holders to prevent misinterpretation. Licensing terms should safeguard against commercial abuse while facilitating academic openness.

With properly designed interactive platforms, shastric learning can move beyond space and time limitations while retaining intellectual rigor and spiritual depth, making ancient traditions relevant in the digital age.

- **Open-Source Knowledge Platforms for Global Access**

Open-source knowledge platforms are democratized means of exchanging indigenous knowledge, dispelling restrictions that belong to proprietary systems and allowing for open-ended contributions by various stakeholders. For IKS, such platforms can be used as living repositories, constantly added to by researchers, practitioners, and custodians of communities.

An open-source knowledge ecosystem finds its base in open architecture. Material digitized manuscripts, academic commentaries, or multimedia are reserved in open formats and tagged with widely comprehensible schemas of metadata. This makes the material compatible across software systems and facilitates an effortless interface with academic databases, digital storage spaces, and educational packages.

Collaborative editing paradigms, similar to open-source software production, can be used for cultural materials. Specialists add peer-reviewed translations, annotations, and cross-links, while members of the public add contextual information and oral tradition. AI-facilitated moderation can provide quality control without suppressing diversity of interpretation.

One of the major benefits of open-source platforms is scalability. With modular architecture, they can support diverse types of resources, high-resolution palm-leaf scans and 3D artifacts, and audio recordings of recited chants and oral histories. Integration with semantic web technologies can facilitate intelligent search, where users can ask questions about philosophical concepts, ritual practices, or historical figures and get networked results that cross several disciplines and locales.

Open-source licensing schemes, like the Creative Commons, enable sharing under control, enabling education and research while guarding against exploitative commercialization. This tracks with indigenous data sovereignty principles, where communities maintain agency over the means through which their cultural heritage is accessed and utilized.

In order to achieve maximum global access, platforms may include multilingual interfaces, adaptive streaming for low-bandwidth networks, and modules for offline access. Alliances with universities, cultural institutions, and technology collectives can guarantee that platform governance is participatory and accountable.

The effects of such platforms go beyond preservation; they actively promote innovation. Researchers will create new analysis tools on top of the open data, educators can design rich curricula, and communities can bring back traditions by making them accessible to younger generations in an interactive manner.

In effect, open-source knowledge platforms convert IKS into living, interactive, and world-accessible ecosystems, guaranteeing that indigenous wisdom not just endures but continues to inspire generations to come.

***

Chapter 7 - Faculty Development, Institutional Culture, and Change Leadership

Placing Indian Knowledge Systems (IKS) within higher education is more than redesigning the curriculum; it calls for a shift in the individuals and institutions that impart and retain learning. Academic teachers are the primary agents of this change, interpreting pedagogical doctrine into classroom pedagogy and research productivity. Unless they are actively involved, any IKS project has the potential to be superficial, confined to token courses or ceremonial inclusion, and not a deep integration into academic culture. Just as significant is the overall institutional culture, where attitudes toward innovation, willingness toward interdisciplinary conversation, and tradition-moderity balance play a role. Change leadership then becomes not only an administrative task but a cultural and strategic one that evokes acceptance, cooperation, and ownership of the change.

This chapter discusses three interconnected aspects of IKS integration: capacity building for the faculty, reforming institutional culture, and leadership in facilitating change. It acknowledges that faculty members are not a homogeneous entity; their disciplinary contexts, epistemological traditions, and pedagogical experiences condition their understanding and acceptance of IKS components. Capacity-building initiatives thus need to be customized, providing both an introduction to IKS principles on a foundational level as well as advanced training in research methods, pedagogic design, and intercultural interactions.

Institutional culture, on the other hand, facilitates or inhibits faculty experimentation. Under strict settings, even well-motivated teachers might find it difficult to bring in IKS material without institutional backing or acknowledgment.Thus, culture transformation means aligning policy, incentives, and assessment mechanisms with IKS integration objectives. The transformation also requires institutions to adopt plural epistemologies, enabling the co-existence of shastric knowledge traditions and modern academic disciplines without hierarchical bias.

Lastly, change leadership has to be proactive, transparent, and participatory. Leaders are not only required to describe the vision for IKS integration but also demonstrate the intellectual humility and receptivity essential to linking traditional and contemporary paradigms. Leaders should balance policy mandates, faculty apprehensions, and student aspirations with ensuring that institutional decisions are evidence-based and culturally informed.

The next sections delve into these issues in detail: developing faculty capacity for IKS-infused teaching and research, cultivating fruitful conversations among shastric pandits and contemporary teachers, overcoming institutional inertia and curriculum inflexibility, and conceptualizing experiential programs like fellowships and workshops. All of these measures together attempt to develop a strong ecosystem under which IKS integration is not so much a top-down mandate as an organically supported academic movement.

- **Capacity Building for IKS-Oriented Teaching and Research**

Faculty staff are the pillars of IKS integration. They define how ideas are introduced and understood. Capacity building starts with laying down foundations. Teachers need to first grasp the philosophical origins of IKS. This involves introduction to classical writings, historical backgrounds, and central epistemological designs. The intention is to establish conceptual clarity. Absence of this foundation might turn education superficial.

Pedagogy must also be trained. Teachers require mechanisms for connecting IKS to modern fields. Lesson plans have to be developed that combine old ideas with new examples. Interdisciplinary methods suit the purpose here. Ayurvedic concepts can be taught in medical ethics courses, for instance. Vedic mathematics can supplement quantitative reasoning courses. Innovative curriculum mapping is the requirement here.

Research competence is also necessary. Faculty should be trained in shastric methods as well as in contemporary research techniques. This would involve textual critique, ethnographic field research, and computer tools for studies in heritage. Well-curated archives and translated primary documents are a must. The resources provide the means to delve into original materials.

Peer-learning websites must be set up. Professors across various disciplines can exchange methods and classroom practices. This instills confidence and minimizes resistance. It also helps create an intellectual ecosystem around integrating IKS. Workshops and colloquia are excellent instruments here.

Mentoring also assists in capacity building. Older IKS scholars can mentor their junior colleagues. It ensures continuity and prevents watering down of content quality. Institutions can make formal mentorship programs part of performance incentives. Innovative IKS-based teaching should be rewarded and appreciated by institutions.

Technology is also a significant player. Faculty need to be trained in handling digital archives, online lexicons of Sanskrit, and artificial intelligence-driven translation software. These enhance access to original material and enhance instructional materials.

The process has to be ongoing. One-time refreshers do not do the trick. Annual refresher courses and topical short courses keep faculty on their toes. This is particularly necessary as more research on IKS keeps coming out.

Finally, capacity building is all about competence and confidence. Staff should feel confident to teach IKS without the prospect of misinterpretation. They ought to also be able to carry out significant research within the field. This synergy guarantees IKS is not an add-on but a living component of academic practice. Strong faculty development is the basis for integration that is sustainable.

- **Dialogues Between Shastric Pandits and Modern Educators**

Substantive integration of IKS involves real dialogue. Shastric pandits possess rich textual memory and interpretive ability. Contemporary educators have formal pedagogy and world academic exposure. The two communities tend to communicate in different languages, literal and conceptual. Establishing dialogue begins with trust. Pandits need to feel their knowledge is revered. Contemporary faculty need to feel their frameworks are esteemed. Respect between the two is the starting point.

This kind of conversation is best fostered in formal forums. They may be seminars, translation workshops, or a thematically organized series of discussions. Pandits can describe the source context of an idea. Teachers can propose how it could be included in a contemporary syllabus. This discussion avoids distortion. It also keeps content topical without compromising originality. The process gains from bilingual conducting. Sanskrit terminology needs to be described, avoiding simplification. Contemporary academic jargon should be inducted with gradualness.

Joint teaching models are effective. A course can have both a pandit and a contemporary academic as co-teachers. The pandit can read and explain the original. The academic can connect it to current uses. Students get to enjoy both authenticity and contextualization. This approach also instructs faculty in integrative pedagogy.

Dialogues also need to accommodate epistemological differences. Shastric traditions tend to work from an axiomatic foundation. Contemporary academia prefers empirical evidence. Bridging the gap needs cautious framing. Inquiring shared questions can facilitate it. For instance: "What was originally intended by this principle?" followed by "How does it differ from existing scientific models?" This kind of framing invites reciprocal curiosity.

Institutional commitment is vital. Travel funds, translation costs, and co-teaching stipends should be provided. A common storehouse of discussion results may be established. This is a living archive for subsequent faculty and students.

The final goal is not uniformity but complementarity. Pandits do not have to adopt modern jargon. Scholars do not have to learn all the shlokas by heart. They each give from their strength. Through such conversation, IKS comes into classrooms as a living, dynamic entity. It is not trapped in the past but mobilized for today.

Table III. Shastric–Modern Education Convergence

Core Dimension	Shastric Pandits' Perspective	Modern Educators' Perspective	Potential Convergence Point
Source of Authority	Scriptural canon, oral transmission, lineage validation	Peer-reviewed research, standardized curricula	Integrative content that respects both validation modes
Language of Instruction	Sanskrit, regional classical languages	English, regional modern languages	Bilingual teaching modules with dual terminology
Teaching Method	Oral exposition (pravachan), memorization, commentary	Lectures, digital presentations, experiential learning	Hybrid delivery combining traditional and digital tools
Epistemology	Axiomatic, metaphysical, holistic	Empirical, analytical, specialized	Comparative epistemology courses
Evaluation Criteria	Disciple's mastery of texts and recitation	Exams, projects, research papers	Mixed assessments combining oral and written evaluation

- **Addressing Institutional Resistance and Curriculum Rigidity**

Resistances within institutions towards bringing in Indian Knowledge Systems (IKS) usually emanate from deep-seated academic hierarchies, bureaucratic lethargy, and a very strong embedded dependence on Western-centric curricula. Most higher education decision-makers are wary of integrating IKS because of issues related to academic rigor, concerns for accreditation procedures, and an assessment of the incompatibility of indigenous epistemologies with modern pedagogical models. Curriculum inflexibility exacerbates this, as program structures currently in place do not offer much space for new and innovative modules or transdisciplinary experimentation.

Solutions to these problems must take a multi-layered approach that addresses policy, pedagogy, and perception all at once. The first step is to sensitize academic leadership and faculty members to the applicability and modern relevance of IKS via seminars, exposure visits, and engagement with subject-matter experts. Presenting case studies where IKS has been successfully incorporated into STEM, management, and social science education can discredit the myth that it is restricted to cultural or historical fields.

Reforms in the administration need to concentrate on the provision of flexible credit systems, electives in learning, and cross-listed courses so that students can be exposed to IKS without any compromise to degree programs. Meanwhile, strategic policy compatibility with organizations like the University Grants Commission (UGC) and the National Education Policy (NEP) 2020 will be helpful in offering a formal adoption framework, making sure that IKS modules have national standards and meet quality benchmarks. The most important aspect is faculty training since instructors need content expertise as well as methodological strategies to impart IKS effectively in contemporary classrooms.

Multidisciplinary course design teams comprising Shastric scholars, modern subject matter experts, and instructional designers can develop academically sound and contextually applicable content. Resistance is often alleviated when faculty members understand that integration of IKS can complement, not substitute for, traditional knowledge areas. Development of interdisciplinary research clusters based on IKS themes also has the potential to promote innovation and outside funding, creating an external incentive for institutions to adopt change.

Curriculum review committees must be authorized to test IKS-integrated courses on an experimental basis, measure results, and replicate successful models. Institutional rewards, through awards, promotions, and research grants, can also encourage faculty and administrators to engage directly in this change. Lastly, constant communication among academic governance bodies, faculty representatives, and IKS specialists ensures that reforms will continue to be adaptive and responsive to criticism. With time, these consistent and sustained efforts have the potential to convert resistance into adoption, making IKS integration a force rather than a contention.

- **Designing Fellowships, Workshops, and Immersion Programs**

Formulating fellowships, workshops, and immersion courses for Indian Knowledge Systems (IKS) calls for a vision that reconciles classical depth with contemporary relevance. Fellowships must be designed to draw scholars from various disciplines to delve deeply into primary materials, oral heritages, and living practitioners of IKS. Such programs need to provide mentorship both from Shastric adepts and contemporary academic supervisors to guarantee scholarly rigor as well as critical discourse. Fellowships of longer duration can be devoted to research and curriculum design, whereas shorter ones can be allocated to applied work, for example, digital archiving or developing teaching materials.

Workshops provide a point of entry for faculty, students, and professionals without any prior experience of IKS. Workshops can range from covering the basic ideas, pedagogic approaches, and applications in a specific discipline, Ayurveda in the health sciences to Vastu Shastra in architecture. These workshops should be interactive in nature, with lectures going hand-in-hand with practical exercises, group discussion, and intellectual debates to promote both intellectual stimulation as well as practical knowledge.

Immersion programs, on the other hand, provide experiential education in real contexts. Participants can spend time in gurukuls, clusters of crafts, or traditional ecological locations to experience the living passage of knowledge. These experiences foster cultural understanding, strengthen conceptual precision, and induce creative means of incorporating IKS into contemporary curricula. Logistical preparation is critical for these programs to be successful. Collaborations with cultural institutions, research centers, and community organizations guarantee exposure to authentic resources and surroundings.

Financial planning needs to be strong, with sources including government grants, private patronage, and international cultural exchange initiatives. Precise outcome measures, like research papers published, curriculum modules prepared, or community initiatives started, are needed to gauge impact and obtain long-term support. Technology can expand scope and reach by supporting hybrid models, where onsite immersion is supplemented by online mentoring and collaborative digital platforms.

Attention should also be paid to creating programs inclusive of diverse socio-economic, linguistic, and disciplinary groups. Evaluation systems must incorporate participant comments, peer review of products, and longitudinal monitoring of how fellows and participants implement their learning in professional practice.

Through the provision of formal opportunities for intense engagement, skill development, and cross-cultural conversation, fellowships, workshops, and immersion programs become drivers towards mainstreaming IKS across higher education and beyond.

They not only provide training to individuals but also develop institutional capacity, making sure that the mainstreaming of IKS shifts from occasional efforts to a persistent and systematic movement.

***

Chapter 8 - Institutional Case Studies and Emerging Best Practices

The embedding of Indian Knowledge Systems (IKS) in higher education is no longer a marginal experiment but an unfolding mainstream movement. Universities all over India, from Indian Institutes of Technology (IITs) to central and state universities, were embedding IKS in teaching, research, and outreach. This embedding is not coherent across all; it varies depending on institutional culture, resource availability, faculty strength, and local community outreach. Some projects target curriculum development, integrating IKS viewpoints into engineering, management, and social science courses. Others specialize in indigenous knowledge research, documentation, and publication in mainstream academic styles.

Private universities and grassroots innovation networks have provided another level to the ecosystem. Contributions from them tend to include agile, community-focused initiatives, online platforms, and entrepreneurial strategies that link conventional knowledge with market requirements. These models are adaptive, responsive, and scalable, which makes them responsive to socio-economic conditions. They also close the space between university research and actual application, making sure that IKS is not just retained but practiced as well.

Globally, comparative experiences focus on both challenges and opportunities. China, Japan, and South Korea are examples of nations that have incorporated indigenous systems, be they traditional medicine, craft, or philosophy, within national education and innovation policies. These frameworks provide significant lessons for India, especially in terms of aligning IKS with contemporary governance, sustainability, and technological integration.

This chapter investigates institutional practice in case studies with practical instances of successful IKS integration. It investigates the varied responses of IITs, central and state universities, and private institutions, as well as grassroots models of innovation. It also provides comparative lessons from national and international experience to derive common factors of success and possible pitfalls.

Synthesizing lessons from experience in policy implementation and practice at the field level, this chapter seeks to develop a reference framework for policymakers, administrators, and educators. It seeks out best practices that can be replicated, adapted, or scaled to fit various institutional settings. It becomes apparent through this investigation that mainstreaming IKS is not an event but a process taking many years, which demands strategic planning, institutional commitment, and cultural sensitivity. The case studies provided here not only capture the scope of experimentation but also highlight the value of a shared vision for fostering indigenous wisdom in the contemporary knowledge economy.

- **IKS Integration at IITs, Central, and State Universities**

- **Background:**

  From niche research since NEP 2020, Indigenous Knowledge Systems (IKS) in Indian higher education have transformed into institutional attention, embedding cultural heritage in sustainable technologies, health, and social innovation. IITs, Central, and State Universities spearheaded the change with research cells and curriculum integration.

- **Case Context:**

  Adoption of IKS has gained momentum, guided by priorities of each institution, technology validation at IITs, multidisciplinary extension at Central Universities, and community-based applications at State Universities.

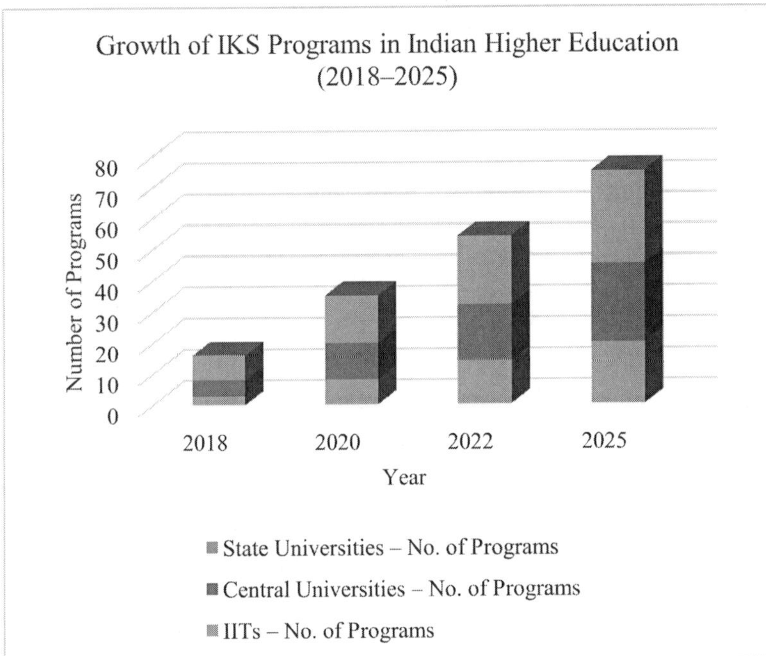

Figure 5. Growth of IKS Programs in Indian Higher Education (2018–2025)

- **Initiatives at IITs:**

  Several IITs have established formal IKS cells or centers. IIT Kharagpur's Centre for Science of Happiness merges Vedic philosophy with organizational leadership training, aiming to create ethically grounded leaders. IIT Delhi's IKS research focuses on engineering applications of traditional water harvesting systems, with prototypes adapted for urban settings. These projects demonstrate how deep-rooted cultural practices can be reframed as modern engineering solutions.

- **Initiatives at Central Universities:**

  Universities like Jawaharlal Nehru University (JNU) and Banaras Hindu University (BHU) have promoted IKS integration across faculties. BHU's Faculty of Ayurveda is working in tandem with engineering departments to digitalize traditional herbal remedies for diffusion. JNU's Department of Linguistics has undertaken projects to document and conserve India's endangered languages, connecting them with cultural and ecological knowledge contained within oral heritage.

- **Initiatives at State Universities:**

  State Universities have rooted IKS in grassroots realities. Rajasthan University's effort to revive johad (ancient water bodies) couples historical accounts with satellite imagery to restore viable systems. Kerala University's environmental science department has collaborated with agriculture cooperatives to marry indigenous crop rotation practices with overall climate change resilience. Such community-linked initiatives place State Universities in central positions as facilitators of transmission from scholarly study to community application.

- **Outcomes and Impact:**

  Since 2018, IKS initiatives have expanded exponentially with higher research funding, online archives, and community collaborations. IKS will become a mainstream element of higher education in India with international applicability by 2025.

- **Private Institutions and Grassroots Innovation Models**

- **Background**

  Indian private universities use flexibility and entrepreneurial spirit to take forward Indigenous Knowledge Systems (IKS) from cultural conservation to market-focused and people-led innovations.

- **Case Context**

  Educational institutions such as Amity, Ashoka, KREA, SRM, and VIT incorporate IKS into specific labs, inter-disciplinary programs, and commercialization streams, bringing fieldwork together with contemporary technology for scalable solutions.

- **Grassroots-Centered Models**

  One of the most impactful strategies is the "University–Village Innovation Loop," originally developed by a group of private technical universities in Gujarat and Maharashtra. Here, students and professors collaborate directly with local artisans, healers, and farmers to co-design prototypes. For example, a water filtration system based on bamboo, embedded in tribal craftsmanship, was re-designed with layers of bio-sand for greater purification efficiency, paving the way for large-scale installation in rural schools.

  Equally, SASTRA University's partnership with Tamil Nadu temple architects has resulted in eco-friendly urban design prototypes based on Vastu Shastra principles from ancient times, reimagined for contemporary apartment buildings. The method combines computational simulation with classical spatial orientation strategies to enhance airflow and energy efficiency.

- **Innovation Pipelines**

  BITS Pilani and O.P. Jindal Global University incubators offer seed capital, mentorship, IP guidance, and industry connections to IKS-based startups, leading to patents, technology transfer, and social enterprise spin-offs.

- **Community Empowerment and Impact**

  The effects of these models are seen in enhanced livelihoods, local employment generation, and the restoration of heritage craftsmanship. By situating indigenous practices within a global system of innovation, private institutions have both enhanced their social value and ensured the ownership of local actors. Grassroots partners are not viewed as passive sources of knowledge but as co-researchers, influencing the design and application of projects.

  Between 2018 and 2025, the number of formal IKS-linked grassroots innovation programs in private universities has increased at a faster rate than in public universities, thanks in part to their flexible governance systems and access to philanthropic support.

- **Outcomes and Impact:**

  Private institutions have shown explosive growth in grassroots IKS programmes between 2018 and 2025, resulting in higher commercialization of indigenous technologies, sustainable supply chains, increased community capabilities, and IKS integration across domains ranging from architecture to artificial intelligence.

- **Comparative Study of National and International IKS Initiatives**

- **Background**

  Comparative context of Indigenous Knowledge Systems (IKS) identifies that whereas India's efforts are rooted in cultural renaissance and vocational training, international equivalents, especially in New Zealand, Canada, and Australia, incorporate IKS into governance, environmental management, and economic self-determination contexts. This offers a worthwhile cross-learning and uptake opportunity.

Table IV. Key Comparative Metrics of National and International IKS Initiatives

Parameter	**India**	**New Zealand**	**Canada**	**South Africa**
Policy Support	NEP 2020, ministry schemes	Mandates on Mātauranga Māori	Reconciliation framework	Indigenous Knowledge Policy
Funding	State + CSR	Govt + Māori trusts	Govt + provincial grants	Govt + research councils
Curriculum	Select universities & hubs	Fully embedded in curricula	Limited to select programs	Agriculture & ethnobotany
Community	Field projects & heritage work	Co-governance with Māori	Community-led partnerships	Joint research & tourism

- **Policy Ecosystems**

  In India, the National Education Policy (NEP) 2020 and the Ministry of Education's IKS Division have commissioned university-level IKS cells, supported research, and advocated skill-based curricula. In New Zealand, Mātauranga Māori is not just an educational subject but a co-governance principle used in resource management, law, and public policy. Canada's First Nations Education Acts formalize Indigenous language maintenance in conjunction with curriculum requirements. Australia incorporates Aboriginal viewpoints in land management through its Indigenous Ranger Program.

- **Funding Mechanisms**

  India combines government grants, Corporate Social Responsibility (CSR) money, and university-initiated seed funding. Canada and Australia, on the other hand, maintain Indigenous programs through trust funds, revenue sharing of natural resources, and treaty allocations, ensuring stability independent of political cycles.

- **Curriculum and Pedagogy**

  Indian institutions have increasingly incorporated IKS into STEM, architecture, and design courses in innovation labs and field studies. In New Zealand, all major subjects incorporate compulsory cultural competency modules. Canada and Australia place a high value on co-developed curriculum content, where Indigenous peoples co-write teaching materials to avoid cultural misrepresentation.

- **Community Participation Models**

  India's University-Village Innovation Loop brings students and artisans together for prototype creation. Community councils co-decide on research projects, intellectual property rights, and benefit sharing in Canada. Australia's on-country training combines ecological knowledge with contemporary conservation science.

- **Key Insight**

India is progressing quickly in the scaling of IKS programs by innovation and commercialization, but foreign models lead in legal recognition, joint governance, and secure long-term funding. The best future for India's IKS might be a combination of its innovation momentum with institutional stability and community autonomy found overseas.

- **Lessons from Policy Implementation and Field Practice**

- **Background**

Successful IKS implementation relies on taking policy ambitions and grounding them in community-led, reality-based outcomes. Observations from India's practice, benchmarked against international examples, yield strategies for long-term sustainability and real impact.

- **Lesson 1: Integration Rather Than Tokenism**

Institutionalizing IKS into mainstream curricula, as New Zealand does through accreditation standards, seeds long-term capacity. In India, shifting from non-mandatory electives to mandatory interdisciplinary modules would enhance cultural transmission.

- **Lesson 2: Predictable and Secure Funding**

Short-term grants place a constraint on continuity. The Canadian multi-decade Indigenous trust fund model can encourage Indian policymakers to create similar endowments, making programs survive longer than political terms.

- **Lesson 3: Co-Design Led by Communities**

  Indian and Canadian projects demonstrate greater adoption when communities co-design research and have control over knowledge ownership. This minimizes dilution of culture and maximizes relevance.

- **Lesson 4: Technology as an Augmenter**

  India's AR/VR heritage mapping and Australia's ecological data platforms are evidence that technology complements traditional practices, not overrules them. Successful instances focus on people's consent and digital skills.

- **Lesson 5: Adaptive Policy Frameworks**

  One-size-fits-all policy prescriptions cannot match the linguistic, ecological, and cultural diversity of contexts. India's regional differences and Canada's tribal self-governance arrangements indicate that adaptive frameworks are most effective.

- **Impact Reflection**

  Where policies are shared by government, communities, and academic institutions, outcomes comprise increased retention of skills, sustainable livelihoods, and an increased sense of identity. Practice in the field shows that capacity-building, intellectual property rights, and economic linkages are necessary for IKS to thrive in both local and global environments.

***

Chapter 9 - Intellectual Property, Knowledge Justice, and Ethical Innovation

The convergence of intellectual property (IP), knowledge justice, and ethical innovation is among the most urgent debates in modern knowledge economies, especially when working with Indigenous Knowledge Systems (IKS). These systems, based on centuries of cultural tradition, oral history, and community-based innovation, are frequently overlooked in dominant global IP paradigms centered on codified, written, and commercially patented knowledge. This asymmetry between TK and modern innovation law gives rise to tensions between the protection of TK and the institutions of modern innovation law, resulting in risks of misappropriation, biopiracy, and cultural erosion. To address this, states and societies are increasingly calling for institutions that protect TK while facilitating fair participation within global innovation systems.

In the Indian case, efforts made under the Traditional Knowledge Digital Library (TKDL) and the National Innovation Foundation (NIF) have attempted to codify, document, and protect community-owned knowledge from exploitative patents. Such protection mechanisms, however, need to be supplemented with knowledge justice principles, knowledge holders both maintaining ownership and also accruing material and cultural benefits from its use. The task is to integrate Western IP regimes, where ownership by individuals and exploitation by the market are prioritized, with Indigenous epistemologies that conceptualize knowledge as an intergenerational, collective trust.

Ethics-based innovation models, especially for IKS-based inventions, call for a change from extraction to co-creation. Examples include the incorporation of Ayurvedic concepts in contemporary nutraceuticals or the evolution of Vastu Shastra in eco-friendly urban planning, proving that innovation can flourish where it is based on cultural sustainability. Such models call for compliance with benefit-sharing arrangements, prior informed consent, and culturally appropriate adaptation of knowledge, as advocated by the Nagoya Protocol on Access and Benefit Sharing.

In times of globalization and online sharing, deprivatizing knowledge access is just as important. Open-source media, community-run repositories, and electronic heritage collections can facilitate TK to continue to be available for education while also being protected from improper use. It is to redefine innovation to prioritize cultural richness, ecological balance, and social justice along with technological progress. This new definition requires new policy priorities, international accords, and moral guidelines that look at knowledge not only as a marketable commodity, but rather as a common legacy to be preserved, respected, and renewable used.

- **Protection of Traditional Knowledge and Indigenous IP Rights**

Traditional Knowledge (TK), ingrained in the cultural tradition of Indigenous peoples, is centuries' worth of established wisdom, covering agriculture, healing, craft, and harmony with nature. Much of this knowledge is shared and passed down through communities, as well as transmitted orally, making it precarious under present intellectual property (IP) regimes that favor written, individual ownership with temporal specificity. The urgent task is to have in place a system that at once keeps off exploitation and promotes fair benefit sharing.

One of the most dramatic examples of protective action is the Turmeric patent case of the 1990s. An American patent had been issued for the antiseptic use of turmeric, a use much recorded in Ayurvedic literature. India challenged the patent, and through a successful demonstration of prior art, had it revoked. Although this was a potent model of defensive protection, it also served to highlight the larger need for proactive strategies that avoid exploitative patents ahead of time instead of responding rear-guardedly.

India's Traditional Knowledge Digital Library (TKDL) provides one such guard against it. It codifies systematically the formulations in Ayurveda, Siddha, Unani, and other Indian traditional medicine, converting them into forms searchable for patents. Consequently, patent examiners around the globe are less inclined to allow patents on existing knowledge from the cultural commons.

At the global level, the Nagoya Protocol, which is an extension of the Convention on Biological Diversity, aims to institutionalize prior informed consent (PIC), mutually agreed terms (MAT), and benefit-sharing mechanisms. This recognizes that knowledge-holding communities' rights go beyond conservation they encompass control over commercialization, cultural integrity, and ecological responsibility.

Even these steps are inadequate if they impose Western legal blueprints on Indigenous epistemologies. Legal scholars advocate sui generis systems, which fit local customary practices, so that communities can delineate ownership, access, and use of TK according to customary norms. Some nations, New Zealand and Peru are examples, are testing these systems, including Indigenous co-governance rights and community registries.

One strong academic discussion by Graham Dutfield points out the multifaceted process of building uniform international protection for TK. He stresses that over-generalization of TK threatens policy incoherence as well as inadvertent marginalization of custodial communities, emphasizing the need for flexible, localized protection measures (Dutfield, G. and Suthersanen, U., 2024)

- **Ethical Frameworks in Shastric Invention and Practice**

Shastric traditions, based on India's rich corpus of classical knowledge systems, include fields like Ayurveda, Vastu Shastra, Sthapatya Veda, Jyotisha, and metallurgy. Shastric systems are not just storehouses of technical knowledge, they represent deeply rooted ethical values that permeate invention, practice, and dissemination. In contrast to modern models of innovation, which tend to emphasize speed, marketability, and competitive positioning, Shastric systems combine scientific understanding with moral accountability, social stability, and environmental harmony.

Underpinning these systems is the perception of knowledge as sacred and required to be used for lokasangraha, the benefit of the world. Invention is not viewed as a solo activity but as a perpetuation of a line of wisdom transmitted through the ages. Ethical limits are inherent in the methodology itself, so that innovations are aligned with dharma (correct duty) and are not destructive to the community or nature. This worldview is a far cry from today's intellectual property regimes, in which protection and gain tend to take precedence over ethical responsibility.

A good case in point is the ancient metallurgy technique of Wootz steel production, famous for its high quality and historically utilized in the legendary Damascus blades. Ancient texts not just detail the technical method, choosing the appropriate ores, smelting under exacting conditions, but also prescribe ethical norms. These involved the procurement of materials with minimal environmental degradation, with decent labor conditions, and limiting the transfer of certain methods to persons who showed honesty and a sense of communal gain. The secrecy was not for monopolization but to keep it out of malicious hands.

Equally, in Ayurveda, new herbal preparation development is based on stern ethical principles. Professionals are bound by codes that exclude the use of preparations for purposes other than healing or gaining personal benefit at the cost of public well-being. The Charaka Samhita, for example, upholds the healer's duty to provide services without bias and to put patient interests first before material benefit.

In contemporary situations, such Shastric norms provide insightful lessons for a reconsideration of policy on innovation. They draw attention to incorporating environmental care, fair access, and moral obligation into the development cycle of an invention from origin to use. As technology advances, going back to such values may give a counterpoint to models that are purely profit-oriented, leading innovations that are sustainable as well as socially equitable

Finally, the Shastric methodology to invention and practice is not one of limiting creativity but of directing it to purposes that promote harmony between human society, nature, and the cosmos. In an age of accelerating technological change, these universal ethical principles can inform a more responsible, culturally embedded model of innovation.

- **Democratizing Knowledge Access in a Globalized World**

With global interconnectedness, knowledge democratization has evolved as both a need and a challenge. The increased velocity of information exchange through digital media has generated unprecedented opportunities for learning, innovation, and collaboration.

But the same globalization tends to magnify inequality, where the availability of key knowledge is unequally distributed because of economic, linguistic, cultural, and geopolitical divides. Real democratization is not simply about providing access to knowledge but also access, comprehension, and usability by various communities without exploitation or exclusion.

Traditionally, knowledge was usually restricted to specific castes, guilds, or academic circles, denying it its potential for transformation. The contemporary digital age, in principle, collapsed many of these barriers, but in practice, there exists a digital divide. Major portions of the international population remain without dependable access to the internet, devices that are not too expensive, or the ability to read, required to interact with a wealth of online information. Furthermore, the prevalence of some languages, such as English, over international knowledge bases marginalizes immense pools of local and indigenous knowledge.

A significant case in point is the Open Access Movement, which has opened up scholarly publishing by lifting scientific literature paywalls. Initiatives such as the Public Library of Science (PLOS) and Plan S have opened scholarly research up to anyone with an internet connection. This has particularly been a boon for scholars and students in developing countries who were once unable to afford subscriptions. Open access is not without its pitfalls, though predatory journals take advantage of the system, and infrastructural disparities continue to keep many at least partially out.

In indigenous knowledge, democratization has to be handled with caution. While making traditional medicinal information available on the internet may aid the global development of health solutions, it is open to cultural appropriation and biopiracy unless safeguards are instituted. The example of the Indian government's Traditional Knowledge Digital Library (TKDL) is one such instance where ancient medicinal texts in various languages have been digitized and placed online for use by patent examiners across the globe to avoid wrongful claims. This system equals openness with protection, balancing the benefits of traditional knowledge to mankind with safeguarding the rights of those communities that keep it.

Actual democratization of knowledge in a globalized world calls for a multi-faceted approach: filling the digital divide through infrastructure development, encouraging multilingual content to embrace marginalized languages, and creating ethical frameworks respecting cultural ownership and promoting global cooperation. That way, knowledge can become an accessible shared resource that enriches societies and does not widen existing disparities.

- **Redefining Innovation through Cultural Sustainability**

Innovation has traditionally been synonymous with technological progress, market revolution, and the development of entirely new products or systems. While this traditional understanding tends to neglect the cultural aspects that determine societies' perceptions of progress, cultural sustainability introduces innovation as a process that not only stimulates economic development but also maintains, renews, and incorporates cultural heritage in modern development. It is in this way that innovation is not simply about producing the new but about making sure that transformation is significant, just, and consonant with the values of those groups it impacts.

Globalization has fast-tracked the dissemination of ideas and technologies, but it has homogenized cultural landscapes and threatened traditional knowledge and practices. Cultural sustainability reverses this tendency by situating innovation in the social, historical, and ecological contexts of society. It believes that cultural heritage, whether as language, art, architecture, agricultural practice, or healing system, is not fixed but dynamic and can be adapted and renewed.

One such successful example is the resurgence of millet agriculture in India. For years, millets, nutrient-dense, water-saving grains, were displaced by industrial farming for wheat and rice. The change undermined indigenous knowledge of farming and lowered the diversity of diets. In recent years, though, agri innovators, policy champions, and grassroots groups collaborated to bring back millets through farmer cooperatives, city retail outlets, and food innovation. By combining conventional farming methods with innovative supply chains, they have developed an economically sustainable, climate-resilient food system that also boosts cultural identity and responds to contemporary nutritional and environmental needs.

This illustration shows that innovation is capable of flourishing by honoring and enriching ancient wisdom without displacing it. Cultural sustainability in innovation promotes hybrid methods, with indigenous practices being legitimized by science, re-interpreted for modern times, and disseminated through shared frameworks. These models promote innovation that does not displace communities from their roots but instead empowers them to meet the future on their terms.

To redefine innovation in this manner, policymakers, educators, and innovators need to embrace a system that appreciates cultural diversity as much as technological advancement. The funding institutions must fund projects that merge preservation of heritage as part of development objectives, while intellectual property regimes need to protect the ownership of culturally sourced innovations by communities. By aligning innovation with cultural sustainability, societies can create pathways that honor the past, serve the present, and remain viable for future generations, proving that progress and preservation are not opposites but mutually reinforcing forces.

***

Chapter 10 - The Future of IKS in Global Academia

The destiny of Indigenous Knowledge Systems (IKS) in international academia lies in reenvisioning education as intercultural, pluralistic, and collaborative. For centuries, the international academic system has been dominated by Eurocentric paradigms that tend to marginalize epistemologies at the local level to mere objects of anthropological inquiry and interest, as opposed to living knowledge systems with an ability to construct the future. As we journey deeper into the 21st century, there are global challenges, ranging from climate change to biodiversity decline, that are demonstrating that monolithic, siloed models of knowledge production are not enough. We need a paradigm shift in which IKS is recognized as not an add-on field, but as one of the pillars of global intellectual thought.

This conversion requires what many academics have called a "pluriversal" methodology, an intellectual place that acknowledges the simultaneous presence of various knowledge systems without reducing them to a single homogenized universal form. This methodology guarantees that Indigenous epistemologies maintain their contextual specificity as they participate in cross-cultural discussions that promote global problem-solving. As Ana Sofía Rojas points out in her 2024 book From Universal to Pluriversal: Transforming Human Rights Education Policies in Colombia, transcending universal to pluriversal approaches in education policy is not merely a matter of philosophical inclination; it is a means toward breaking down systemic disparities and creating true intercultural learning spaces. This vision is in harmony with the wider mission of incorporating IKS into curricula not as esoteric case studies but as coequal sources of theory, method, and innovation.

Within global academia, the recognition of IKS must also account for power imbalances in knowledge production. Although academic publishing, peer review processes, and research funding tend to function under dominant epistemic principles, institutional reform can infuse equitable collaboration as a core value. South-South collaborations, multilingual publishing platforms, and open-access research repositories are some structural reforms necessary to enhance the visibility and reach of IKS.

In addition, the usage of IKS principles is not limited to cultural heritage; it provides essential input to sustainability science, climatic resilience, and people-led innovation. The international academic environment, reconstituted using a pluriversal framework, has the potential to be a living database where Indigenous ways of knowing drive new technologies, ecological stewardship, and socio-economic policy.

In the end, it will take institutional courage, epistemic humility, and policy architectures that look at diversity not as a problem to be contained but an asset to be scaled. This chapter navigates these opportunities, contending that IKS inclusion is not just an act of remediation, it is a strategic imperative for creating a more sustainable, just, and intellectually rich global knowledge society.

- **Towards Pluriversal Education and South-South Collaborations**

The pluriversal principle erodes the deeply held conviction of a unitary, universal structure of knowledge. Rather, it celebrates a world where diverse epistemologies coexist, maintaining their cultural integrity while sitting in meaningful conversation with one another. For Indigenous Knowledge Systems (IKS), such a paradigm provides a critical escape from the fringes of the academy and takes an equal seat with dominant Eurocentric models. Pluriversal pedagogy acknowledges that the knowledge inherent in local languages, oral culture, and cultural practices is not additive, it is central to constructing robust, fair, and place-specific responses to collective challenges.

South–South partnerships are a natural extension of the pluriversal imagination. These partnerships unite countries in Asia, Africa, and Latin America, places where IKS is still thriving but frequently under-prioritized in school curricula. Through horizontal interchanges as opposed to hierarchical ones, South–South partnerships can steer clear of extractive dynamics sometimes implicated in North–South academic partnerships. Co-creation of curriculum, research methods, and innovation platforms that respond to similar histories of colonial defiance, environmentalism, and cultural diversity is possible through such partnerships.

Mechanisms for such partnerships necessitate deliberate frameworks. Shared research institutes, inter-institutional faculty exchange programs, and multi-language publication channels can facilitate the weakening of language and cultural frontiers. For instance, an Indo–Brazilian knowledge exchange on agroecology may bring Ayurvedic farming principles together with Amazonian permaculture practices to yield hybrid models appropriate to varied ecologies. Likewise, synergistic climate adaptation measures between South African and Indian coastal communities may combine traditional meteorological wisdom with contemporary data analytics and develop resilient early warning systems.

Importantly, pluriversal education is not an abandonment of scientific rigor, it is an expansion of what counts as rigorous knowledge. The recognition of oral narratives, community mapping, and participatory observation as valid academic contributions democratizes the process of knowledge production. This, in turn, cultivates intellectual humility, a quality essential in a century where uncertainty and complexity are the norm.

If taken up en masse, pluriversal learning and South–South partnerships would redirect world academia away from a center, periphery to a system of interconnected, mutually valued systems of knowledge. Through this process, it would not merely shore up the value of IKS but also diversify world problem-solving with a multiplicity of viewpoints that one single epistemic tradition could not possibly generate by itself.

- **Building a Sustainable IKS Ecosystem for the 21st Century**

Sustainability in the context of Indigenous Knowledge Systems is broader than environmental; it includes cultural continuity, intergenerational knowledge transmission, economic sustainability, and institutional resilience. The construction of such an ecosystem is necessary, in which IKS is seen as a living and developing body of knowledge instead of a dead remnant from the past. This means a transition from preservation as an end in itself to preservation as a basis for innovation.

A sustainable IKS system is based on three interrelated pillars: community stewardship, academic integration, and technological enablement. Community stewardship assures that the knowledge keepers maintain agency over how their customs are preserved, transmitted, and modified. Academic integration entails integrating IKS material across the disciplines, not as ghettoized electives but as essential parts of science, engineering, law, and governance curricula. Technological enablement implies using digital technologies to facilitate preservation and dissemination, while avoiding cultural appropriation.

Digitization, for example, can render rare manuscripts, ancient medical recipes, or traditional indigenous farming calendars to a worldwide audience. But such initiatives need to be preceded by ethical standards and community approval processes. Intellectual property management through blockchain is also on the cusp of becoming a usable technology to ensure equitable sharing of benefits from commercial uses of IKS, e.g., pharmaceutical research findings, with the communities of origin.

Another essential aspect is economic sustainability. IKS-based businesses, ranging from handicrafts to herbal medicine, can be traced to fair-trade markets, tourism, and climate-resilient agriculture.Universities and research institutions can serve as incubators for these ventures, providing technical assistance without commodifying or watering down cultural content.

Furthermore, a sustainable IKS system should encompass youth engagement mechanisms. Storytelling festivals, gamified learning sites, and experiential field courses have the potential to get younger generations to appreciate and innovate their heritage. This intergenerational transfer maintains continuity while allowing adaptive evolution against contemporary challenges.

In the 21st century, the IKS system needs to be envisioned not as a stand-alone preserve but as part of an active global network. Sustainability will lie in its capacity to feed into, and learn from, the larger reservoir of global knowledge—on equal terms. Nurtured in this manner, IKS is no longer just a heritage commodity but an engine for cultural resilience, ecological stewardship, and socio-economic innovation.

- **Policy Roadmaps and Strategic Recommendations**

For Indigenous Knowledge Systems (IKS) to succeed in global academia, policy has to transcend mere symbolic declarations. It has to seek profound structural integration. This calls for a clear framework for tackling legal safeguards, educational transformation, research finance, and worldwide collaboration.

A top priority is legal protection. Intellectual property systems have to protect indigenous rights. This involves recognizing collective ownership, which is distinct from traditional patent systems. States like India can enact special IKS protection legislation. These can bring together traditional rights and up-to-date enforcement systems. These systems make sure indigenous communities receive equitable benefits from commercial applications of their knowledge.

The second front of importance is that of education policy. Schools and universities need to integrate IKS into the curriculum. This is more than inserting new content. It is about methodological pluralism. Education needs to incorporate oral histories, community-based field work, and cross-disciplinary projects. Teacher training needs to equip educators to mediate between knowledge systems. It needs to eschew stereotyping or exoticization of indigenous cultures.

Third, the funding of research should be redirected. Special grants for IKS-related research should be developed. National science institutions can develop special funding lines. International funds for IKS research can be provided by several nations and philanthropic organizations. This guarantees resources for preservation and innovation.

Global policy alignment is as much needed. Frameworks like UNESCO, the African Union, and BRICS can spearhead pluriversal education charter leadership initiatives. Such agreements can establish common norms for cross-border IKS integration. South–South research networks, supported by diplomatic and trade alliances, can facilitate long-term collaborative efforts with secure funding and assessment systems.

Evaluation and monitoring need to be integrated into each phase. Measurement should not just count outputs, such as the quantity of IKS courses. It should also monitor outcomes like the well-being of communities, biodiversity preservation, and innovation uptake. This maintains the attention on real impact over symbolic participation.

A strategic policy framework for IKS has to harmonize preservation and progression. It has to honor local ownership while participating in a global partnership. It has to preserve cultural integrity while facilitating economic gain. With the support of political will and community alliance, these policies can move IKS to the forefront of sustainable global development.

Table V. Summary of the Five Pillars: Focus Areas and Outcomes

Pillar	Focus Area	Expected Outcome
Data Integration	Unified collection and linking of multi-source data	Consistent, reliable data foundation
AI & Analytics	Predictive and prescriptive modeling	Improved decision-making accuracy
User Experience	Intuitive, accessible interfaces	Higher adoption and user satisfaction
Security & Privacy	Data protection and compliance	Enhanced trust and regulatory adherence
Scalability	Modular and adaptable architecture	Sustainable growth and performance

- **Reimagining Indian Higher Education Through a Civilizational Lens**

India's higher education system is at a critical point in history where the desire to be a world leader in knowledge comes up against the necessity to scrutinize academic priorities. While major advances have been made towards increasing access, quality, and research productivity, the intellectual riches inherent in India's civilizational heritage, ranging from Vedic, Buddhist, Jain, Islamic, and varied regional traditions, are still underexploited. Reconceiving Indian higher education in civilizational terms means not just incorporating pieces of traditional wisdom into curricula, but integrating them into the fabric of research, teaching, and institutional life.

Ancient universities like Takshashila, Nalanda, and Vallabhi illustrated cosmopolitanism of scholarship, where philosophy, astronomy, medicine, governance, and arts were studied integrally. Knowledge crossovers and learning were situated in moral, ecological, and social contexts. Restoring this ethos in contemporary academia requires deconstructing narrow disciplinary compartments and encouraging integrative modes. For example, integrating Ayurveda with modern biomedical sciences can provide innovative healthcare models for various populations, and reconciling Vastu Shastra with green architecture can feed climate-resilient urban planning.

The National Education Policy (NEP) 2020 offers a strategic window for such shifts, supporting multidisciplinary education, nimble curricula, and research systems. But achieving this vision is not just a matter of policy phraseology—it necessitates training faculty in transdisciplinary approaches, strong investments in Indigenous Knowledge Systems (IKS) research, and the development of specialist centers that harmonize tradition with advanced technologies such as AI, biotechnology, and climate modeling. Civilizational knowledge must be viewed as a dynamic, living resource—reinterpreted again and again to suit current needs—instead of being a fixed cultural relic saved only for symbolic purposes.

Internationalization efforts also have to be reimagined. Collaborations with other ancient knowledge traditions like Chinese Confucian scholarship, Egyptian engineering tradition, or Andean agricultural knowledge can give rise to comparative studies that enrich global discourse on sustainability, ethics, governance, and epistemology. Such efforts place India not as a subservient follower of global knowledge trends but as a co-contributor that is helping forge a pluriversal scholarly order.

However, there are structural issues still to be addressed: over-dependence on Western models of accreditation, a lack of institutional support for IKS research, and under-representation of indigenous thinkers on decision-making organs. These can only be resolved with radical reforms, including the creation of independent IKS universities governed by community-based participation and socially oriented mandates.

Finally, by basing its higher education system on a civilizational perspective and adopting contemporary research methodology, India can build a bridge between the legacy of the past and the changes of the future—both fortifying its indigenous intellectual ecosystem and contributing to a genuinely inclusive global knowledge society.

***

References:

Kumar, M. and Pandian, S., 2023. Harmonizing indigenous knowledge systems to the Indian educational philosophies for quality education: a review study. *World Journal of Advanced Research and Reviews*, *21*(3), pp.2177-2185.

Sen, S., Barman, M., Majumdar, S., Bala, A. and Das, T., 2025. HOLISTIC APPROACHES TO LEARNING INSPIRED BY GURUKUL SYSTEM AND ITS PRESENT IMPORTANCE. *Archives*.

Innocente, C., Ulrich, L., Moos, S. and Vezzetti, E., 2023. A framework study on the use of immersive XR technologies in the cultural heritage domain. *Journal of Cultural Heritage*, *62*, pp.268-283.

Dutfield, G. and Suthersanen, U., 2024. Traditional knowledge as intellectual property subject matter: perspectives from history, anthropology, and diverse economies. In Handbook of innovation and intellectual property rights (pp. 270-290). Edward Elgar Publishing.

Rojas, A.S., 2024. From Universal to Pluriversal: Transforming Human Rights Education Policies in Colombia. *Current Issues in Comparative Education*, *26*(2), pp.57-76.

***